Introducing Theology to Laity

A Challenge to the Whole Church To Explore God's Nature

John Wesley Zwomunondiita Kurewa

Africa Ministry Series

Introducing Theology to Laity

Cover Design: Marc Whitaker/MTWdesign.net; Karin Wizer
Cover Photo: Shutterstock
Typesetting: PerfecType, Nashville, TN

ISBN: 978-0-88177-899-1

This book is dedicated to the laity and clergy
of the whole church in Africa.

Contents

Preface

It all started with a conversation between my brother and me. My younger brother and his wife were visiting my wife and me in our home. I was part of a family of ten children: three girls and seven boys. All three sisters are still living, as are two brothers—my brother who is three years younger than me, and me. Having been raised in a Christian family, each time any of the five of us visit each other, our conversations are often centred on our families, extended families, the church, and national or international issues. This time my younger brother, who is an active layperson in our village local church, brought up a bus accident that killed about ten passengers and injured a good number of the others. After our discussion of the tragic incident, my brother summarized all that we had discussed by saying, "Well, that shows when your time to die has come, there is nothing you can do about it."

"You mean all those who perished in the accident had been scheduled to die on that same day?" I asked. I challenged my brother to explain.

"Yes. What can we say? God has assigned each one of us a time when we have to die; and when that time comes, no one can say no," my brother affirmed.

Knowing that this was a common belief of many Christians, some of whom quote the words of the "Teacher" of Ecclesiastes who states, "There is a time for everything, and a season for every activity under the heavens: a time to be born and a time to die," (Eccles. 3:1–2), I deliberately took some time to discuss this theological issue with my brother.

"There could be another way of looking at the issue, my brother," I said. "God may not be so concerned that none of us overstays beyond the date we were intended to die to the extent that so many people would have to be killed in a bus accident."

"Well, those who escaped death in the accident clearly had not yet reached the end of their time; and those who died had, and could not escape," my brother asserted.

"So, you believe all ten died because their time was up; and that even if they had not been on the bus, they would have died anyway?" I asked.

"Most likely," he said.

Knowing that my brother is a good driver, I asked him, "Is it not likely that most of the accidents that occur, among many other reasons, are caused either by human or mechanical error?"

For instance, in Zimbabwe we drive on the left side of the road. Suppose I was driving along the road, and indicate I am turning to the left, but end up turning to the right, and am hit by a car that intended to overtake me on my right side. That is a human error that could cost me my life. How would someone turn round and say, "The accident occurred because it was the time for John to die?"

"Does that make any sense?" I asked. I went on to explain that as human beings we live in the solidarity of life both in good as well as in evil. Suppose I had two or more passengers in my car. It would mean two or more people might also die with me in the accident because of my human error. So the passengers suffer, even suffer death with me, because of my human error. Such an accident could also have been caused by a mechanical error—an undetected faulty directional indicator that signalled I was turning in the opposite direction. That also could cause death to both the driver and the passengers. Does it really make sense to turn round and say, because God had already assigned a time for John and all the people John thought he was helping by providing transport, they all have to die together in a car accident? That would almost mean God planned the accident, wouldn't it? And what kind of God would that be? Certainly, not the New Testament God!

As my brother listened attentively, I added, "When an accident occurs, our attitude should be that of the Good Samaritan, as taught by Jesus. The injured must quickly be attended to and despatched to the nearest hospital for healing and comfort" (Luke 10:25ff).

"The dead," I said, "we assume, like Lazarus, who at his death was taken to Abraham's bosom (Luke 16:22), will also be taken to a place of rest and comfort from unbearable agony of body and spirit and the horrendous experience of the accident. They will become God's people, as John says, '"He will wipe every tear from their eyes. There will be no more death' or mourning or crying or pain, for the old order of things has passed away" (Rev. 21:4).

"Thanks, brother! I never thought of it that way," my brother said. "You clergy people need to teach us more about these things." His words challenged me to see that theology is not only for the clergy; the study of theology should be for the whole body of Christ—the church.

This conversation with my brother motivated me to write this book. I did not write of a theology that has been adjusted for the laity. Rather, I wrote the book in the spirit of encouraging the laity to read and study theology as the clergy do. Consequently, this book explores the doctrines of God, creation, humanity, sin, the problem of evil and God's providence (Theodicy), Christology, the Holy Spirit, the Trinity, the Atonement, the church, mission of the church, ministry, sacraments, and eschatology.

In this book, chapter 12, "Historical Development of the Ministry," is a recast of part of my earlier book *Drumbeats of Salvation in Africa* (chapter 5, "Evangelism in the Early Church," 2007). In view of the rise of numerous prophets on the continent today, it is important to acquaint the laity of similar developments in the early church, and how the early church responded.

Chapter 1

What Is Theology?

Theological talk is part and parcel of our daily conversation. In the Shona culture of Zimbabwe one often hears the statement, "*Zvaitika pano, kana Mwari haafari nazvo,*" meaning, what has happened here, even God is not happy. Christians and non-Christians alike talk theology on a daily basis. A white farmer once said to me, "John, you go to church to pray, and I don't. However, each morning as I wake up and walk around my farm, I look up to heaven and wonder whether God is going to send us rain or not." He was not simply praying for rain to come; he was also talking theology.

Defining Theology

The word *theology* is a combination of two Greek words: *theos*, which means "a god or deity, God,"[1] and, *logos*, which means "a word, a saying, statement, declaration, thought or speech, discourse, teaching doctrine,"[2] or study, or rational thought. Thus, strictly speaking *theology* means a thought or study about God and all his activities in the universe (Gen. 1:1–3:24, Ps. 24:1–2, John 1:3, Col. 1:16). However, one may need to ask some more questions.

First, what is theology as a discipline or subject of study? We shall turn to a few definitions:

1. Four scholars who co-authored *Christian Word Book* wrote, "Theology is the study of God. A theologian is a person who studies God. Theologians try to make as clear as possible what it means to use language about God. Theology does not have to be Christian. A Christian theology studies God as He is known through Christ. Since the church

witnesses to Christ, the theologian is: (a) a person who has faith in God through Christ, and (b) one who takes part in the church."[3]

2. "Theology may be defined as the study which, through participation in and reflection upon a religious faith, seeks to express the content of this faith in the clearest and most coherent language available."[4]

3. "Systematic Theology is the critical discipline devoted to discovering, expounding and defending the more important truths implied in the experience of the Christian community."[5]

4. Daniel Migliore quotes Anselm, a twelfth-century archbishop of Canterbury, who taught that "theology is . . . faith seeking understanding."[6] In other words, theology for Anselm was the means or instrument with which faith sought understanding. Let me illustrate.

In one remote, rural church school in Zimbabwe, the teacher discovered that one of her pupils had a charm tied on his arm. The discovery created commotion in the classroom. The teacher forcefully removed the charm from the pupil's arm. Immediately, the child left the classroom screaming, "*Mandibvisira wasekuru wanondicheneta*!" The meaning is: "You have removed the ancestors, who look after me." Within two hours, the family members of the pupil came to see the headmaster about the incident. The family was annoyed with what had happened and tempers were running high. Since I was the pastor of the area, living within the proximity of the school, the headmaster immediately called me in to be an intermediary between the teacher and the offended family of the pupil.

What I discovered were two religions, each with a different object of its faith. On one hand, the family of the young man felt insulted by the teacher who removed the charm from their child, for they claimed the charm protected not only the young man but also the whole family. The family had faith in the charm, for the charm symbolized the enshrined ancestral spirits—the object of their faith. On the other hand, the teacher believed in Jesus Christ, who was the object of her faith. Thus, there emerged a theological crisis of the two faiths. It helps to remember that theology does not have to be Christian. Neither does one person force another person to be converted to his/her faith. However, for Christians theology is a critical means of understanding the Christian faith.

Others have said, "Theology is the language of religious faith."[7] It is the study of a particular faith or religion with a view to understanding by exhibiting its distinctive and unifying themes.

Second, what is the relation between faith and theology? Or are theology and faith the same thing? It is common to hear some students of theology say, "When I came to this theological institution I lost my faith because of the theology it teaches." There might be some truth in that statement, but theology and faith are two different things, though related. Faith, *fide* in Latin and *pistis* in Greek, can be understood in two senses: (a) Faith may be understood as a relationship between a person and the object of faith. For Christians the object of their faith is God. "Have faith in God," Jesus said (Mark 11:22). One who does not believe in God may have other objects of faith such as power or wealth, or fetish, as we noted above. (b) "In the second sense, faith may mean the contents or set of beliefs a person holds. Such use is implied in saying, 'He believes in the Christian faith,'"[8] or he believes in the Islamic faith or the Jewish faith.

It needs to be stated at the outset that the object of theology is the study of one's faith. As much as we may say even as Christians that theology is the study of God, God is not a thing to be scientifically investigated. Rather, what theology investigates is people's faith in God. Our faith is more tangible as it is expressed both in our personal and devotional life, as well as in the corporate statements and doctrines that we believe as the community of faith. The tangible phenomena of faith consist of praying regularly, studying the Bible, attending religious meetings, giving offerings, and familiarizing ourselves with doctrines. Such religious phenomena are what theology investigates. And, such Christian religious phenomena enable the theologian to understand what the Christian community believes about God.

Third, what is the relationship between doctrine and theology? In the New Testament Greek the word is *didache*, which means "that which is taught (Matt. 7:28, Titus 1:9, Rev. 2:14, 15, 24"[9] or "what is taught, teaching, act of teaching, instruction."[10] The English Bible uses the word *doctrine* or teaching or instruction. For example, Paul writes to Timothy, "Watch your life and doctrine closely" (1 Tim. 4:16); and to Titus, "You . . . must teach what is appropriate to sound doctrine" (Titus 2:1). Below are four definitions of doctrine.

(a) "Doctrine is a set of teachings accepted by a group of persons who are followers of a particular ideology or philosophy."[11]

(b) "Christianity also speaks of its doctrines but has one supreme doctrine—God known in Christ through the Holy Spirit."[12]

(c) "Christian doctrine is not a system, but a life; and Christian doctrine is the interpretation of a life . . . Christian doctrines are an attempt to express in words of formal statement the nature of God and Man and the World, and the relations between them, as revealed in the person and life of Jesus."[13]

(d) Doctrine is "the content of the Christian message in the thought of our day."[14]

Therefore, doctrine is the end result of a theological investigation of faith and what is to be taught to the members of the church. However, doctrine will never graduate from the investigation of theology, for every generation of believers must also raise questions concerning doctrines they inherit from previous generations.

Akin to doctrine is *dogma*. Philip Watson says dogma is "the religious interpretation or elaboration of an experienced historical fact or event . . . Dogma is essentially expression, declaration, proclamation; it is a kind of preaching, a form of the Word of God."[15] "How it happened is wholly outside the realm of our experience; that it happened is not, and the fact that it happened is what the dogma declares . . . Dogma, let it be said again, is a religious expression of religious experience; it is a declaration of faith and nothing else."[16] Watson points out three fundamental dogmas—those of Creation, Incarnation, and the Resurrection.[17]

Formative Factors of Theology

John Macquarrie apparently coined the phrase "formative factors in theology."[18] He also said that these formative factors in theology could not be "all on the same level or of equal importance."[19] Some Church of England scholars of the eighteenth century were already aware of some of the formative factors. Those of the Methodist Christian heritage got to know four of them as Wesley's Quadrilateral: scripture, tradition, reason, and Christian experience.[20]

Macquarrie gives a list of six formative factors in theology, which include:

1. *Experience.* Experience appears first, "because theology implies participation in the religious faith."[21] Experience in a religious faith comes first, for the life of faith precedes theology. Experience comes by participating in a community of faith. This experience may include moral struggle and intellectual quest, and experience in many other aspects of life.

2. *Revelation.* Revelation is the primary source of theology. Revelation translates the Greek word *apokalypsis*, which literally means "an uncovering, a laying bare, making naked."[22] John Baillie says, "Revelation literally means an unveiling, the lifting of an obscuring veil, so as to disclose something that was formerly hidden." To disclose means to uncover, but in ordinary usage it does not mean to discover.[23] As a technical-theological term, it is commonly said that there are two basic models for understanding revelation. For the Roman Catholic and Christian Orthodox generally, revelation is "disclosure of a series of supernatural truths."[24] The Protestant view says that revelation is "a disclosure not of propositions but of God himself."[25] Hence John Baillie says, "There is no such thing as revealed truth. There are truths of revelation."[26] God is the content of revelation. He is the one who discloses or uncovers himself as he did to Moses in a burning bush (Exod. 3:2),

and Isaiah in the Temple (Isa. 6:1–13), and to Philip (John 14:9). This may be understood by some as *special revelation*, while *general revelation* occurs through the common experiences of mankind available in many lands and throughout the ages.[27] It is important to remember that ideas concerning revelation are common to all religions.[28]

3. *Scripture.* The scriptures play a large part in Christian community, and therefore are a significant source of theological reflection. The scriptures themselves are not revelation; rather, they testify to the revelation of God, which culminates in Jesus Christ. For Christians this is true of both the Old and New Testaments. Jesus is quoted saying, "These are the very Scriptures that testify about me, yet you refuse to come to me to have life" (John 5:39–40). That means both the Old Testament and New Testament testify to Christ; the former says he will come, and the latter says he has come and will come again. Hence, Dwight Stevenson says, "Before you can preach from the Bible you should settle the question of the relation of scripture to the Word of God. To be fuzzy at this point is to confuse the preaching ministry from start to finish."[29]

4. *Tradition.* Roman Catholics have always held the view that "the revelation of Christ has been transmitted to us both through scripture and tradition, while the Protestants have acknowledged the scripture alone."[30] Properly understood, tradition is no rival to scripture, but is its necessary complement.[31] John Macquarrie reminds his readers, especially Protestants, that the "earliest Christian scriptures were preceded by and based upon tradition that was handed down and in turn received in the primitive Christian community, as is made clear by St. Paul"[32] (1 Cor. 11:23, 15:3).

5. *Culture.* If theology is to sound intelligent it has to use the language of culture. In Africa, theology has to learn to use African thought forms and idiom—the language, folk tales, proverbs, riddles, and the like. Culture is communication. As people in worship express themselves in songs and other culturally oriented ways, likewise theological

reflection needs to be expressed in the same manner. As long as African Christians continue worshipping through western rituals and styles, it becomes harder for them to theologize through other people's experiences, traditions, and cultures.

6. *Reason*. There has been a tendency by some theologians to exclude human reason in theology. Such theologians suggest that theology rests purely on revelation, i.e., on God's disclosure alone. The truth of the matter is that as one is encountered by God's disclosure, reason begins to relate that revelation. "Woe to me!" cried Isaiah, "I am ruined!" (Isa. 6:5); or as Paul rightly asked, "Who are you, Lord?" (Acts 9:5). Reason is an integral source of doing theology.

Branches or Divisions of Theology

We have been talking of theology in an undifferentiated way. But it is essential to know that there are branches or divisions of theology. It is important to see how these branches or divisions of theology relate more than they differ from one another.

First, Daniel Migliore gives us the following branches of theology:

1. *Biblical theology*, which studies in detail the canonical writings of the Old and New Testaments that are acknowledged by the church as the primary witness to the work and word of God.

2. *Historical theology*, which traces the many ways in which Christian faith and life have come to expression in different times and places.

3. *Philosophical theology*, which employs the resources of philosophical inquiry to examine the meaning and truth of Christian faith in the light of reason and experience.

4. *Practical theology*, which is concerned with specific tasks of ministries of the church such as preaching, education, pastoral counselling, caring, and other ministries.[33]

Second, Macquarrie lists the following divisions of theology:

1. *Philosophical theology*, which he says is "descriptive rather than deductive [from general to particular], and performs the function of

providing a link between secular thought and theology proper. It lays bare the fundamental concepts of theology and investigates the conditions that make any theology possible."[34]

2. *Symbolical theology*, by which he means "the unfolding and interpretation of the great symbols or images of faith in which the revealed truths of faith are set forth—the triune God, creation, the fall of man, incarnation, atonement, eschatology, and whatever else belongs to the specific faith of the Christian Church."[35]

3. *Applied theology*, which is "concerned with the expression of faith in concrete existence in the institutional, cultic and ethical aspects of the life of the faith."[36]

Macquarrie presents his divisions of theology with the assumption or understanding that "apologetics, biblical theology, and historical theology are not distinct branches of theology, but special ways of considering theological questions, and clearly the pronouncements of both biblical and historical theology must be carefully considered over the whole areas of symbolical and applied theology."[37]

That having been said, both Migliore and Macquarrie seem to be saying the discipline that we study as theology rightly is systematic theology. Migliore does so by saying that in his book "we take up that aspect of the larger theological task of the community of faith, which is called *systematic theology* (also called doctrinal, constructive theology)." As systematic theology is constantly informed by other theological disciplines, its main task is "to venture a faithful, coherent, timely, and responsible articulation of Christian faith."[38] Similarly, Macquarrie also talks of systematic theology as "the total theological enterprise as this has been unified by the architectonic [having structure or design] reason,"[39] and that systematic theology "seeks to articulate all the constituent elements of theology in a coherent whole, and that it seeks to articulate this whole itself with the other fields that go to make up the totality of human knowledge, and especially with those disciplines which stand in a specially close relation to theology."[40] Both Migliore and Macquarrie do not consider systematic theology as a branch or division; rather, they see it as the total theological task that pulls together all branches or divisions of theology to articulate the Christian faith timely and responsibly.

The Task of Theology

Often, theology "grows out of the dynamism of the Christian faith that incites reflection, inquiry, and pursuit of the truth not yet possessed, or only partially possessed."[41] In terms of the function of theology:

First, theology is a critical instrument of the church. "Actually all theology is critical."[42]

Second, Gustaf Aulen says the object of theology

> is to understand the faith. Systematic theology has as its object of study the Christian faith. The intention of the discipline is to elucidate the content and meaning of the Christian faith with all the means at its disposal. The task is . . . analytical and critical. Its purpose is neither to furnish proofs nor to determine what "ought to be believed." Every thing is concentrated on the attempt to understand the faith and to present its meaning with the greatest possible clarity.[43]

Third, again, the object of theology is faith. God is not a thing to be scientifically investigated; rather, theology investigates faith—that living relationship in God.

Fourth, "Theology, as a function of the Christian church, must serve the needs of the church. A theological system is supposed to satisfy two basic needs: (a) the statement of the truth of the Christian message, and (b) interpretation of this truth for every new generation. Theology moves between two poles, the eternal truth of its foundation and the temporal situation in which the eternal truth must be received."[44]

Fifth, Philip Watson says that the task of Christian theology "is to show what Christianity is, not to prove that Christianity is true."[45]

Theological Method

Some theologians have been associated with distinctive theological methods—Rudolf Bultmann with demythologizing, Paul Tillich with correlation, and Karl Barth with dialectic.[46] For instance, Tillich says, "Systematic theology uses the method of correlation . . . [which he defines as] theology formulates the questions implied in human existence, and theology formulates the answers implied in the divine-manifestation under the guidance of the questions implied in human existence."[47] Barth's method of theology is "*Christocentric* theology or theology of the Word of God . . . [Thus] Barth describes theology as a discipline of the church in which the church continuously tests itself and its proclamation by its own norm, which is Jesus Christ as attested in Scripture."[48] Marcus Ward does not give a name to his theological method, but he says that "in the study of each doctrine, the main emphasis shall be on the biblical foundation of that doctrine . . . and a short historical study of the doctrine . . . Finally, on the systematic side the object shall be to explain the generally accepted Christian position with regard to each doctrine . . ."[49]

African theological methods differ somewhat in regards to participation, interpretation, and dialogue. The following is a recast of part of my article, in an abbreviated form, "The Meaning of African Theology," published in *Journal of Theology for Southern Africa* 11 (July 1975).

1. *Participation*. African theology takes place in the context of a Christian community. This means that an African theologian (be he/she black, yellow, or white) must fully participate in the African Christian community where faith and life express themselves. In fact a theologian must belong to a Christian community where he/she participates in its worship, mission, and any other church activities. This gives one

the opportunity to reflect upon the faith as well as helping lead this faith to further clarification.

There are other qualifications an African theologian will need to meet. He/she will need to be a person who fully participates in the African experience(s). This African experience has no formula other than being African, or at times Black. To this day, to be Black is synonymous with what we call African experience. Therefore, it is the African or Black, alone, who has "certain impressions, judgements, feelings and perceptions that others do not share."[50] Additionally, an African theologian should be a person who participates in African culture. This point is important because as I have mentioned culture is communication. It is often out of the culture of a people that a communicating theologian will find structures or thought-forms, method, and intelligible and meaningful expression of the Christian faith.

2. *Interpretation*. While a theologian is a participant in a religious community and should enjoy the religiosity of the community like anyone else, at the same time he/she will need to keep his/her head above the religiosity excitement of the community. He/she must never forget that there is always a further step to go; a theologian must keenly observe and precisely describe what goes on in the community to which one belongs. At this point, an African theologian would do well to pay attention to phenomenology of religion—"a method which seeks to ascertain what religion is by identifying, understanding, classifying and describing appearances (phenomena) of the religions."[51]

3. *Dialogue*. As much as African theology is an attempt to emphasize the reality of the Christian faith on African soil, dialogue with the rest of Christendom needs be maintained because African theology itself is part of the whole and therefore cannot isolate itself from one faith that Christians declare in Christ Jesus. African theology needs a dialogue with other young theologies such as Black theology (USA), Yellow or Asian theology, theology of liberation in Latin, Red theology

(USA), and others of similar background. It also needs a dialogue with older theologies such as European Continental theologies and American theologies, to mention a few. Finally, African theology needs consistent dialogue with the theologies of different periods of Christian thought—beginning with Biblical theology, Patristic theology, Monastic theology, Scholastic theology, Confessional theology, Denominational theology—for in all this treasury lies a great tradition for the whole of Christendom, from which African theology cannot dare to be isolated.[52]

Chapter 2

The Making of the Bible

It is essential that all Christians know something about how the Bible was made or came into being. The entire Bible (sixty-six books) was written over a period of a thousand years. Some of its authors will never be known to us. Given the period in which the Bible was written, it is obvious the authors neither knew each other, nor knew that what they were writing would one day be considered authoritative scriptures. In Christian theology, the Bible is the primary source of information concerning Christianity; and therefore, the Bible becomes the normative source for our study of theology.

Making of the Old Testament

The Old Testament consists of assorted documents that were composed over a period from about 1200 to 100 CE.[1] Take note of the reference to CE, the Common Era, and BCE, before the Common Era.[2] Harrell Beck informs us that "from the time of the patriarchies [Abraham, Isaac, Jacob] there were many popular histories, poems, and religious teachings circulating in Israel. Many such traditions and teachings were circulating both orally and in written form from the time of David (about 1000 BCE) onward."[3]

In examining a rough outline of the chronology of the writings of the Old Testament, C. H. Dodd commented,

> You will observe that not one of the books of the Old Testament (in its finished form) is of earlier date than the eighth century BC. Before that time there existed

> traditions handed down by word of mouth, and various documentary records and compositions, which were used by later writers. But the books of the Old Testament, as we know them, were composed in the period starting with the great prophets Amos [750–744 BCE], Hosea [745–734 BCE], Isaiah [740–700 BCE] and Micah [700 BCE]. And it was the work of these prophets which directly or indirectly determined the character of the Canon of Scripture. Their stamp is in one way or another upon it all.[4]

There occurred what is known as the canonization of the Deuteronomic Code—the first notable event toward the canonization of the Old Testament in 621 BCE, when in the process of renovating and cleaning the temple, the high priest, Hilkiah, "found the Book of the Law" (2 Kings 22:8). That was the beginning of the canonization process or making of the Old Testament. One may ask, What is canonization?

> The English term "canon" comes from a Greek word that originally meant "ruler" or "measurement rod." A canon was used to make straight lines or to measure distances. When applied to a group of books, it refers to a recognized body of literature. Thus, the canon of Shakespeare refers to all of Shakespeare's authentic writings. With reference to the Bible, the term canon denotes the collection of books that are accepted as authoritative by a religious body. Thus, for example, we can speak of the canon of the Jewish Scriptures or the canon of the New Testament.[5]

Additionally, the word *canon* means a rule, or authority or standard that was used to determine acceptability of the books of the Bible as authoritative over the community of believers. Out of numerous books that had been written, only the thirty-nine books in the Old Testament, and twenty-seven books in the New Testament were canonized or met the standard; hence, the reference to the books of the Bible as canonical books. The process of canonization, both for the Old Testament and the New Testament books was "gradual and controversial."[6]

The army of Sennacherib, king of Assyria, which had already overrun Phoenicia, Samaria, and all towns of Judah, then invaded Jerusalem. Sennacherib described Hezekiah king of Judah "like a caged bird, shut up in Jerusalem, his royal city" in 701 BCE.[7] Hezekiah was desperate. Isaiah acted and advised Hezekiah not to capitulate to Sennacherib's threats on basis of "a royal theology which developed in Jerusalem under the influence of Nathan's prophecy to David. This oracle (2 Sam. 7), it will be recalled, announced Yahweh's *unconditional promise* to maintain the Davidic throne, regardless of the merit or demerit of Israel's kings."[8] Therefore, for Isaiah:

> Zion would not fall . . . Yahweh's saving purpose in history was tied up especially with the city of Jerusalem. For Jerusalem was the place of the Temple, in which the Ark rested. Jerusalem was the city Yahweh had founded (14:32); Mount Zion was "the place of the name of Yahweh of hosts" (18:7). It was in Jerusalem's Temple that Isaiah had seen the vision of Yahweh, the King. Moreover, Jerusalem was the City of David. And the Davidic dynasty, which had survived through three troubled centuries of history, was the sign of a special stability that Yahweh himself had given.[9]

The prophet Micah who prophesized between 750 and 668 BCE and therefore was a contemporary of Isaiah, and had predicted the fall of Samaria (Mic. 1:6), which took place in 722–721 BCE),[10] rebuked the leaders and false prophets during the invasion by Sennacherib: "Therefore because of you, Zion will be plowed like a field, Jerusalem will become a heap of rubble, the temple hill a mound overgrown with thickets" (Mic. 3:12). While Isaiah did not disagree with the message of Micah that catastrophic destruction was coming soon to Jerusalem, Mount Zion, and the Temple, and the need for repentance by Israel, he happened to look beyond the ensuing disaster. He cast his eyes ahead and perceived the "remnant of Israel" that will return and rely only on the Lord (Isa. 10:20). It was in this light, primarily of the remnant, that Isaiah delivered the Lord's message to Hezekiah, "I will defend this city and save it, for my sake and for the sake of David my servant" (Isa. 37:35).[11] Thereafter, an angel of the Lord is reported to have caused the death of 185,000 men in the Assyrian camp. That forced Sennacherib to withdraw and return to Nineveh (Isa. 37:36–37).

> Whatever the true explanation of Sennacherib's sudden withdrawal, the event made a deep impression upon Judean memory. The fact that Yahweh had spared Jerusalem in that crisis came to mean in popular thought that Yahweh would spare Jerusalem under any circumstances. Zion would stand forever![12]

The people of Israel relished that popular theology that Yahweh would protect or defend Mount Zion and Jerusalem for his name's sake, at the expense of repentance and amendment to their way of life. The years 597 and 587 brought disaster to Jerusalem. The cream of Jewish leadership was taken into captivity by Nebuchadnezzar of Babylon, leaving all the poorer elements of the population behind.[13] Israel never heeded the word of the prophets who proclaimed that God wanted them to change their way of life and follow him. By that time, the city of Jerusalem had been destroyed, the temple was in ruins, and the people were in a foreign land, wondering if their God, Yahweh, had been defeated by a foreign God. Israel had been left with nothing to hold on to for their faith and worship. "By the rivers of Babylon we sat down and wept when we remembered Zion . . . How can we sing the songs of the Lord while in a foreign land?" (Ps. 137:1, 4).

The destruction of Judah in 587 BCE and the long Babylonian exile began the search for something that would give Israel a sense of authority over its life and people. Thus the canonization process that began with King Josiah in Jerusalem in 621 BCE was revived once more.

First, the *Pentateuch*, 400 BCE: The word *Pentateuch* refers to the first five books of the Old Testament. Tradition has always ascribed the authorship of the books to Moses, but modern scholarship does not, although certain specific passages are attributed to him (Exod. 24:4, 34:27, Num. 33:2, Deut. 31:9, 22, 24–26).[14] These five books are also known as the Law of Moses (Torah in Hebrew). The Samaritans held only these five books as their scriptures.[15]

For the Jew, "the Pentateuch is the heart of the Old Testament—'the Law.' All else is commentary and elaboration."[16] We have already pointed out that most of the tradition was passed down from one generation to another by word of mouth, in the form of narratives, poems, proverbs, riddles, and most likely laws. Centres such as Bethel and Shechem in the North and Beersheba and Hebron in the South are where some written traditions were likely to be found. By 400 BCE, the priests had put together a great body of legal tradition, the Torah. The Book of Nehemiah chapters 8–10, the Torah, was read to the people of Israel by Ezra about 400 BCE,[17] and the people accepted it as authoritative over Israel. Thus the Pentateuch was canonized.

Second, the *Prophets*, 200 BCE: Two centuries before the Babylonian Exile, the prophets had preached and warned Israel about the impending disaster. Thus, between 500 and 200 BCE both the national history and the oracles of the prophets were brought together on scrolls.[18] The books of history, four scrolls that covered the period from the invasion of Canaan down to the exile, were called Former Prophets—Joshua, Judges, 1 and 2 Samuel, 1 and 2 Kings. All the prophetic oracles in

Israel were also brought together in four scrolls (Isaiah, Jeremiah, Ezekiel, and the Book of the Twelve or Book of Minor Prophets). By the year 200 BCE all these writings had been accepted as part of the Hebrew Bible—a second part of the Bible.[19] Thus this second part of the Bible had become canonical.

Third, the *Writings*, 90 CE: A council of rabbis met in Jamnia, a coastal Palestinian town, for the purpose of closing the canon of the Hebrew Bible, by approving the Writings.[20] Luke quotes Jesus saying, "Everything must be fulfilled that is written about me in the Law of Moses, the Prophets and the Psalms," (Luke 24:44), leaving out the rest of the books of the Writings, because they were not yet part of the canonical Hebrew Bible.

Making of the New Testament

Like the Hebrew Bible, the collection of early Christian writings and their canonization was a long and gradual process. The New Testament contains twenty-seven books, and it was written in Greek between the years 50 and 120 CE.[21] It was not until the fifth century that the twenty-seven books officially became canonical scriptures. The New Testament consists of two parts: (1) There are four Gospels that proclaim the good news by narrating the story of the life, ministry, death, and the resurrection of Jesus of Nazareth. Two of the Gospels were written by Matthew, former tax collector (Matt. 9:9), and John, the son of Zebedee (Mark 3:17). The other two Gospels were written by John Mark, who served as the secretary of Peter, and Luke, the physician and companion of Paul on his travels. There is the book of Acts, commonly believed to have been written by Luke, the physician. Essentially, Acts serves as a bridge for the writings of the New Testament. It narrates the beginning of Christianity and its spread in Jerusalem and the whole of Judea, to Samaria, and to the Gentile world including Rome, the capital of the Roman Empire. (2) Then, there are twenty-one books, which originated as writings by the apostles to the churches: some to the churches the apostles had founded, and others to the Christian communities universally. Out of the twenty-one books, Paul is believed to have written thirteen of them.[22]

The twenty-seven New Testament books were not the only Christian writings; there were many more. It was only through the process of canonization that the church came up with the final twenty-seven. In canonizing the twenty-seven New Testament books, four points are critical to the process.

First, the central event of each book is that *Jesus as God* had come into the world—*Jesus is the Messiah.*

Second, the early Christians took on a new perspective and understanding of *the Hebrew Bible.* The Jesus-event had fulfilled the Hebrew Bible. Thus the Hebrew Bible became the first canonical scriptures for the Christian church. Adolf Von Harnack says that the Jewish Bible became a hindrance for decades to the creation of the New Testament "because the Old Testament in a very complete and masterly way was subjected to Christian interpretation, and so Christians already possessed in it a foundation document for that new thing which they had experienced."[23]

Third, as Jesus did not leave his church any written documents, the *apostles* played an important part as the representatives of Christ. They were eyewitnesses to his life, ministry, death, appearances after the resurrection, and his ascension (Luke 24:44–48). Thus, the Old Testament and the apostles are witnesses of Jesus.

Fourth, the process of canonization of the New Testament is outlined here:

(a) Around 140 CE, Marcion, a son of a bishop, a wealthy man, and a native of Sinope, a seaport in Pontus, moved to Rome, where he associated himself with the church.[24] He produced the first fixed canon of scripture. He believed that Paul was the only authentic apostle of Jesus Christ. Therefore, he picked up all the ten letters (without the Pastorals) attributed to Paul, and Luke's Gospel, as canonical scriptures.[25]

(b) About 170 CE, the so-called Muratorian fragment or the Muratorian canon showed "a New Testament that contained the four-Gospel canon and an apostolic part, to which belonged incontestably thirteen Pauline epistles, Acts, 1 Peter, 1 John and the Apocalypse."[26]

(c) About 180 CE, Ireneus, Bishop of Gaul, now France, declared that according to God's decree, "Four Gospels are entrusted to the church, not more, not less."[27] He accepted the thirteen Pauline letters, Acts, Apocalypse, 1 Peter, 1 and 2 John. He was undecided on Hebrews, 3 John, 2 Peter, James, and Jude.[28]

(d) The Synod of Laodicea met in 363 CE to resolve the New Testament canon. Subsequently the canon consisted of the following books: the Old Testament and all the books of the New Testament as we know them today, except Revelation.

(e) In 367 CE, Athanasius, the African Archbishop of Alexandria, in his customary Easter pastoral letter was the first church leader to list all twenty-seven New Testament books as we have them today.

(f) The second Church Council to resolve the New Testament canon met in Carthage in 397 CE under the leadership of Augustine, Bishop of Hippo. The Council approved as canonical the twenty-seven books of the New Testament as we know them today; and Rome gave its approval to the recommendation of the Carthage Council in 419 CE. It was the African church council that forwarded the final recommendation to the Pope in Rome for approval of the canonical Bible as we know it today.

The Bible as a Book of Mystery

Many Christians treat the Bible as a book of mystery (mystery in the sense of being unexplainable or unknowable). They refer to the Bible as the Word of God, and the mystery comes in the way God wrote the Bible. The unfortunate result is that many then use the Bible as a charm or a fetish. They associate the Bible with mystical or magical powers. This is demonstrated in the way the Bible may be used in driving away demons. Other examples are when people claim that a house was gutted by fire but a copy of the Bible survived; or a soldier carries a pocket Bible believing that magically it will protect him/her from a bullet. Or a person who has had bad dreams wakes up and puts a Bible under his or her pillow. That is using the Bible magically or as a fetish. A lack of Christian education perpetuates such practices of misuse of the Bible by members of our churches.

The substance of the gospel is the mystery of the Bible. Yet, the mystery surrounding the Bible continues to cloud the minds of many Christians. Admittedly, there is genuine mystery about the good book, but that mystery can be solved in the substance of the gospel itself. George Hendry had this to say about the mystery of the gospel:

> In the NT a mystery is a secret which has been or is being disclosed; but because it is a divine secret it remains mystery and does not become transparent to men. . . . In the Pauline terminology mystery is correlative with revelation. The substance of revelation is the mystery of the gospel (Eph. 6:19) or the mystery of God (Col. 2:2), the divine purpose which was kept hidden from former ages and has been made known in the fullness of the times through Christ (Rom. 16:25ff, Eph. 1:9). To Paul the mystery relates to the inclusion of the Gentiles as well as the Jews in the divine purpose of salvation. (Rom. 16:26, Col. 1:27, Eph. 3:3–6)[29]

Authority of the Bible

Most Christian communities do not question if the Bible has authority for Christian faith; rather, they question where the authority of the Bible lies. Or, what sort of authority is it?

Harrell Beck raised some questions about the Bible: (1) Is the Bible infallible (incapable of error, never wrong)?

> According to Genesis 1, God created all things and finally he created man; according to Genesis 2, God created the earth and heavens, and then he created any other life . . . The Gospels provide differing accounts even of major events in the life and ministry of Jesus. But errors and contradictions do not seriously detract from the basic religious testimony that a biblical passage presents.[30]

(2) Is the Bible morally questionable? "Some of the stories in Judges, Samuel, Ezra, and Nehemiah are characterized by a distressing nationalistic exclusivism . . . the Book of Esther is the slaughter of 75,000 gentiles . . . Psalm 109 is a cry for vengeance against an enemy . . ."[31]

(3) Jesus made corrections when he taught, "You have heard that it was said to the people long ago . . . but I tell you . . ." (Matt. 5:21–22).

Another common view is that the source and authority of the Bible is divine inspiration. People are quick to quote the verse: "All scripture is inspired by God and profitable for teaching, for reproof, for correction, and for training in righteousness, that the man of God may be complete, equipped for every good work" (2 Tim. 3:16–17, RSV).

What is this text saying? The word *inspiration* comes from the Greek word *theopneustos* (*Theos*, God, *pneo*, to breathe).[32] Literally, it means every scripture was "breathed into by God."[33] Because the above statement is an attributive to God, we have to ask ourselves, What does it mean to be breathed into by God?

It is in the interpretation of the above statement that differences have emerged. There are different views concerning the meaning of the inspiration of the Bible: (a) Those who advocate "verbal inspiration of the Bible." This view holds that the Holy Spirit literally dictated the words of the Bible as we have it. The prophets were merely the mouthpiece of God. Such persons may emphasize what they call supernatural origin.[34] The logical conclusion is that if God dictated every word there are no errors in the Bible. Or, the Bible is infallible.[35] (b) Others talk of this divine inspiration as "plenary inspiration," meaning full or complete. This term ensures that "no part of the Bible would be omitted" with regard to inspiration and counters a view that "the inspiration of Scripture can rightly be affirmed of the whole without the parts, or of some parts but without the whole." Underlying this view is a theological belief that the very words of scripture were revealed and inspired by God. It is important to note that nowhere else in the Greek Bible does the term *inspiration* appear.[36] It is also important to note Bruce Metzger's observation about the early fathers of faith when he says, "Nothing was said concerning inspiration"[37] as a criterion during the whole vigorous process of canonization.

Let me share a more excellent and correct view concerning the inspiration of the Bible. According to Harold DeWolf, "Before each part of the Bible was written there were such events in the experience of the writers as to induce the writing. Inspiration is to be attributed primarily to these experiences and only secondarily to the passages in which they found expression."[38]

Similarly, Macquarrie says, "The Bible may be taken perhaps as the basic authority for it has a fixity and objectivity that give the kind of stability that is needed if the community of faith is to preserve an identity. Yet this community of faith is not the community of a book, but a living community. Its faith came before the book, and indeed it was the community which determined the canon of scripture."[39] Hence, Beck says:

> The Bible has come to us from the hands of men. According to their own testimony they were inspired by God and sustained by God. But they were men, born in varying times and circumstances, and their environment affected their writings . . . The Bible is a record of the experiences that men have had when they encountered God. These were vital, redeeming, religious experiences, so full of power and meaning that the persons involved felt compelled to

> share with others the redeeming truth that they discovered . . . The Bible is the record of events of incomparable importance, a fact that would be admitted even by those who have little serious interest in its teaching . . .[40]

Now let us turn to authority of the Bible. This authority is found in the redeeming "acts of God" beginning with what God did in Abraham, the father of faith, and culminating in Jesus Christ. Migliore says, "The Bible is a unique witness to the sovereign grace of God at work in the history of Israel and above all in the life, death, and resurrection of Jesus."[41]

Ernest Wright said that in the Old Testament there are five basic events or "acts of God": (1) the call of the fathers, (2) the deliverance from slavery, (3) the Sinai covenant, (4) the conquest of Canaan, and (5) the Davidic government.[42] One may not agree with some of the acts or all of them, but that is how a faithful Jew understood the history of salvation.

Reginald Fuller said that there were three basic acts of God in the New Testament story: (1) the real life and teaching of Jesus, (2) his death on the cross at the hands of the Romans, and (3) his resurrection as head of the new community established in him—the church.[43] This is the way a Christian understands salvation in Jesus Christ.

Therefore, that which generates the *primary inspiration* in people and brings about faith, or created a living community of the children of Israel long before the canonization of the Jewish Bible, or the Christian community before the canonization of the New Testament, was the most fundamental factor. It is that about which Alan Richardson says, "In authorizing a canon of scripture, the church recognized an authority which it did not create,"[44] namely, the saving acts of God in history that culminate in Jesus Christ.

The Word of God is the authority of the Bible. Necessarily, Jesus Christ is the Word of God. As already indicated above, the revelation of

God through all the saving acts in history culminates in the person of Jesus Christ. That was the reason Jesus said to the Jews, "You study the Scriptures diligently because you think that in them you have eternal life. These are the very Scriptures that testify about me, yet you refuse to come to me to have life" (John 5:39–40). Again, Jesus Christ, the Word of God, is the authority of the Bible.

The Bible is the Word of God because it testifies to Christ, and it is the testimony of those who actually saw and witnessed the saving acts of God in history (Exod. 10:2, 12:26–27, 13:8, 14–15, Deut. 4:34–35, 6:20–23, Judg. 6:13, Ps. 44:1, 1 John 1:1–3). This is the significance of both the Old and New Testaments. Both Testaments witness to the Christ: "The OT contains the testimony of the prophets to the Christ who should come; the NT contains the witness of the apostles to the fact that Jesus of Nazareth is he."[45]

Similarly, preaching becomes the spoken word of God. This is because through our preaching God may communicate his message of love, peace, and eternal life.[46]

Chapter 3

Belief in God

The African people have always believed in God. This is important to establish because some early missionaries from the West assumed that the African people were heathens. The definition of the word *heathen* is "a member of any people not worshipping the God of Israel; anyone not a Jew, Christian, or Muslim; a person regarded as uncivilized, irreligious."[1] Because the God that the African people believed in and worshiped was completely unknown to the western world, they concluded that the African people were heathens.

African Belief in God and His Creation

The belief in one Supreme Being, God, is upheld firmly by African Religion. In spite of all other beliefs of the people throughout sub-Saharan Africa, belief in the one Supreme Being is the most fundamental. The belief in the one Supreme Being, God, is the foundation upon which African Religion is established and must be understood. This belief stands out symbolically as a point of unity for the whole region of sub-Saharan Africa. Further, the task of working toward a united Africa and perceiving of Africa as unitary is not just a political and economic issue; it is also deeply a religious matter for all Africans. For that reason we delight in the knowledge that if there is any one factor that undergirds Africa's unity, apart from the geographical bond of one continent, it is the African peoples' belief in one God.[2]

There is no reason to believe that African knowledge of God as it is understood in African Religion, even prior to the advent of Judaism,

Christianity, and Islam, came from outside the continent. That knowledge of God as Supreme Being was there in Africa from time immemorial. Some Christians believe that God's revelation was limited to the Judeo-Christian tradition alone, excluding other traditions and religions. But we must not forget Amos, an eighth century BCE prophet who claimed to see the Lord standing by the altar (Amos 9:1). The Lord in one of his utterances through Amos, the prophet, said to Israel: "Are not you Israelites the same to me as the Cushites? . . . Did I not bring Israel up from Egypt, the Philistines from Caphtor [generally identified as Crete[3]] and the Arameans from Kir?" (Amos 9:7). This was a message of God through Amos to show Israel that Yahweh had not only revealed himself to Israel or delivered Israel alone from an unbearable historical situation; he had equally delivered other peoples too, such as the Philistines, and the Arameans. Today African Religion scholarship is beginning to unveil signs that indeed the same God had been showing himself to our ancestors; their religious tradition shows that Africans were not heathens as others had often believed and taught. Throughout sub-Saharan Africa, African Religion has confirmed the teaching of God, the Creator of mankind and all creation.

Similarly, the rabbinical tradition held that "the Mosaic law had been proclaimed on Sinai in the seventy languages of mankind, although only Israel hearkened and obeyed."[4] Even if Sinai was not the platform from whence the proclamation went out, it would seem God's self-disclosure to the African people was evident. Two scholars have written passionately about the reality of God for the African people.

First, Bolaji Idowu, a Nigerian theologian, wrote, ". . . there is no place, age, or generation, which did not receive at some point in its history some form of revelation."[5] Therefore, in examining God's revelation with regard to African Religion, Idowu came up with four factors:

(1) "God is real to Africans."[6] An example that demonstrates this reality of God's revelation among the African people is that in "Africa,

each people has a local name for God."[7] (2) "God is unique."[8] To show the uniqueness of God, Idowu shares with his readers this beautiful story:

> In Ido mythology, there is a story that Olokun (the arch-divinity) who is the beloved son of Asanobwa (the Supreme God) was, therefore, vested with all the attributes and glory due to his position. Olokun challenged his Father to a display of splendor and majesty. In accordance with African practice, he chose an open market place for the display. When the appointed day arrived, the Father sent his messenger to tell Olokun that he was ready and that Olokun should meet him at once at the appointed venue. Olokun dressed himself in what he considered to be excellent regalia and came out of his room. Imagine his chagrin when he saw that his Father's messenger was dressed identically as he! This will not do, he thought. He therefore went back into the room and changed his regalia. When he came out again, he found out the messenger had changed identically as he. In the long run, he made a total of seven trials of regalia in order to go out and meet his Father; but each time he was frustrated because the messenger of the Father was identically dressed as he. In the end, he had to give up the attempt, admitting that it was impossible for him to go out and compete with his Father since he could not beat even his messenger in such a display. The Father's messenger was Chameleon![9]

What a story to demonstrate an understanding of the uniqueness of God! The story also shows the genius of African people in their ability to discern God's revelation both in human affairs and through nature. Indeed, the African people perceived God's hand and his uniqueness in human affairs, his creation, and nature. Idowu goes on to say, "The uniqueness of the deity is one reason there are no images—graven or in drawing or in printing—of him in Africa."[10]

(3) "God is the absolute controller of the universe."[11] African people have always believed that God is in complete control of all his creation. While they may speak of God as withdrawn from the people, they also talk of God as one who intervenes to protect the innocent from harm by the evil ones. Thus, for the African people to show that God is in control, he is both a *transcendent* and *immanent* being. He is also *omnipotent.*

(4) "God is one, the only God of the whole universe,"[12] says Idowu. There is no one who could possibly compare with God. It is for that reason that in Africa none of God's personal names are ever used to name a human being. Idowu closes his discussion on what he considers the correct African belief about God with the following quotation of a dialogue from Lloyd C. Douglas:

"What is the word for God?" he asked.

"Which one?" inquired Esther, innocently.

"The only one," he said severely.

"*Theos*," she replied, after a little pause.[13]

Second, according to John Mbiti, from time immemorial African religious tradition has passed down from generation to generation both personal and attributive names of God that sustained African knowledge of God as a Supreme Being. For example, men in Shona villages once sat around a fire after sunset and shared various stories, folk tales, their history, proverbs, and many other things. Once in a while, someone would raise the question, Who is greater *Chidzachepo*, meaning the Stump that has always been there, or *Muwanikwapo*, meaning One who was found already there. Both *Chidzachepo* and *Muwanikwapo* were attributive names of God. That kind of question often provoked a theological discussion that involved most of the young persons sitting around the fire. Meanwhile, the elderly men simply listened, for they knew there was no easy answer as both names referred to the eternal One.

Some people even regarded it a taboo to ask the direct question, Who created God? The African people believed God the Creator was a Supreme Being. However, some of the African ethnic groups preferred to talk of God as having created himself. For example, the Bemba ancestors of the Democratic Republic of Congo called God *Na Luntutwe*, meaning the One who created himself, while the Bemba people of Zambia called him *Shi Shaibumba*, also meaning the One who created himself.

Then, almost all African peoples affirm God as the Creator: the Kimbundu ancestors of Angola called him *Ngana Nzambi*, meaning Creator; the Lunda ancestors of Democratic of Congo called him *Sakatanga*, meaning the Creator. The Bemba ancestors of Zambia called him *Kabumba* (pronounced as *Kawumba*), meaning the Creator; the Timni ancestors of Sierra Leone called him *Kuru-masaba*, meaning God of Creation and Provider of his creation; in Swahili they called him *Mwenyezi Mungu*, meaning Creator of the universe; the Xiswa ancestors of Mozambique called him *Nungungulu*, meaning the Creator; and the Xhosa ancestors of South Africa called him *Umdhali*, meaning the Creator.

Again, each African ethnic group has a name for God that specifically indicates that humanity was created by God. For example: the Luba ancestors of Democratic Republic of Congo called him *Muhangi wabantu*, meaning Creator of people; the Tsua ancestors of Mozambique called him *Muvangi vavanhu*, meaning the Creator of people; the Hausa ancestors of Nigeria called him *Mahandici Kowa*, meaning Creator of people; the Shona people of Zimbabwe called him *Musikavanu*, also meaning Creator of people. Because humanity's livelihood has always been intricately bound together with the natural environment—animals, fish, birds of the air, oceans and rivers, mountains, trees, and grass—it must have led the African people to the conclusion that this was all God's creation, and a manifestation of his incredible greatness as God, the Creator.

There are also anthropomorphic names for God. For example in the Shona culture, there are such names as *Pfuyavarombo*, meaning one who looks after the poor; *Bvuteguru*, meaning a great shade or shelter, where birds of the air, animals of the jungle, and even human beings come to rest or find protection from the heat of the sun. In traditional worship among the Shona people, any reference to God is done more through attributive and anthropomorphic names than personal names of God. This is because attributive and anthropomorphic names are richly endowed with theological expression concerning God's nature and activities among his people. Personal names simply mean God; and unfortunately these are the names missionaries used in Bible translation, with the view to achieve the universality of God among a people. However, all such attributive and anthropomorphic names of God by the African people are a great source of African knowledge about God. Such knowledge is an affirmation that, long before the missionaries came to sub-Saharan Africa, the knowledge of God already existed. What the Africans did not know was the person Jesus Christ, the Son of God.

In addition, there are several African myths that attempt to explain how humanity came into being. For instance, the Shona people of Zimbabwe talk of *Musikavanhu* (Creator of people), who planted a reed at the middle of a pool of water. After some time, the reed burst, and from it came out the first man and the first woman, from whom all humanity filled the earth. This legend of the reed is also shared in Botswana, for Gabriel Setiloane of Botswana wrote about a legend of the Sotho-Tswana, which also alleges that humankind originated "from a bed of reed."[14] Setiloane expanded the idea:

> The legend of man's appearance from the reeds, linked explicitly by BaSotho with Ntswana-Tsatsi is re-enacted at every birth among the Sotho-Tswana as a whole. A reed is placed across the doorway of the hut, in which the mother

> and her new-born child are confined, barring entrance to all but the midwives and other local women who are themselves mothers. Mother and child are "*ka mo lethakeng*" (in the reed); and every individual's birth recapitulates the first emergence of man.[15]

The Luhya people of Kenya teach that humanity came from the knee of God. They explain that God's knee swelled larger and larger and eventually, man popped out.

Essentially, most of the myths that deal with the creation of humanity in Africa indicate that God is either directly or indirectly involved, something that confirms humanity's existence as God's creation. The African people in sub-Saharan Africa do believe in God and that God is the ground of the existence of the universe and all humanity.

Other Views Concerning Creation

There have been all kinds of methods to try to understand humans, their origin, welfare, and happiness in this life. We will examine several of these approaches.

Scientific materialism. This is a worldview that rejects any theistic or supernatural explanation of reality.[16] It challenges the cogency (reason or argument) of the teleological and moral arguments. It argues that the universe needs no supernatural cause or government; it is self-existent, self-explanatory, self-operating, and self-directing.[17] Therefore, humans are a product of natural processes. After all, the earth is not the centre of the universe, the human body has a humble origin, the mind is influenced by many factors, and humans are no more than a highly developed ape. They are like any other animal, and their religion is wishful thinking.[18]

Humanism. This is the quality of being human, or human nature. It is a worldview that acknowledges or is based on human nature, human dignity, and the ideals of humans. Humanism emphasizes that this is the only life you have, so enjoy it. You are meant to be happy and you exist for happiness. You do not need the supernatural in order to live happily. It is defined as "any view in which the welfare and happiness of mankind in this life is primary."[19] Also, "any system of thought or action based on the nature, dignity, and ideals of man; specif., a rationalist movement that holds that man can be ethical, find self-fulfilment, etc., without recourse to supernaturalism."[20] H. G. Wells, the prophet of humanism, "preached the coming of the perfect man through his own powers, released by education."[21] This view appeals to those who have made it in life, not to the poor. Kenneth Kaunda, former president of Zambia wanted to be known as a Christian humanist, which he defined like this: "By Christian humanism I mean that we discover all that is worth knowing about God through our fellow men and unconditional service of our fellow men is the purest form of service of God."[22]

Communism. This political doctrine teaches quite rightly that "men need a power to build them together in community. It meets the problem quite wrongly by an attempt to create a new man, not as an individual, but as a collective personality."[23] Therefore, communism overrides and ignores the value of a person as an individual, as the state becomes paramount.

Christian Belief in God

Christianity affirms belief in the Triune God: "I believe in God, the Father Almighty, creator of heaven and earth. . . . I believe in Jesus Christ, his only Son, our Lord . . . I believe in the Holy Spirit, the holy catholic church, and the communion of saints . . ."[24]

First, Christians believe in the one God (Deut. 6:4, Mark 12:29–31), who reveals himself and is experienced as the Triune God in three manifestations (2 Cor. 13:14). Christianity may speak of doctrines "but has one supreme doctrine—God known in Christ through the Holy Spirit."[25] As Africans, we know something about God, the creator of the universe, all that is in it, and humankind. As Christians it is absolutely essential that we know and understand God as he is revealed in Christ Jesus, and continue to learn of him through the prompting and teaching of the Holy Spirit.

Second, the Christian ground of belief in God may have several layers, that is: (1) from the beauty and order of nature (Ps. 102:25, 111:3, 121:1); (2) from the testimonies of the great characters of the Bible such as Abraham, Moses, David, Amos, Isaiah, John the Baptist, Peter, and Paul; (3) ultimately, the ground of Christian belief in God is ". . . that the testimony of what is held to be the revelation of God to those who have received it and live by it does carry its own guarantee of truth. We know by experience."[26]

A woman was converted in a congregation I served. She was married, and had four children. She also had four demons in her life. In helping the woman go through a conversion experience, I found that it took almost four months for her to say yes to a new life in Christ. As she gave a testimony about six months after her conversion, she shared with the church about the change that had come into her personal life. She shared about the new love she had for her husband and children. Prior to her conversion she testified that she perceived her husband as a stranger in her life and home, and her children as worrisome all the time. After conversion she shared about the love she had acquired in serving her church. Everything about her had changed. She said that for the first time she loved her husband and enjoyed her children as a blessing from God. She was a new creation in Jesus Christ. That is what we mean by knowing God and his love through Jesus Christ.

Christian View of Creation

The Christian view of creation is presented in two traditions, both found in the Book of Genesis. The first tradition is known as the Jahwist (J) tradition (Gen. 2:4–7), and the second one is the Priestly (P) tradition (Gen. 1–2:3). Of the two presentations of creation in Genesis, the Jahwist account is considered the older document than the Priestly document.[27] The Jahwist account simply narrates the story of the Garden of Eden, that Yahweh made earth and heaven and that he formed man from the dust of the ground, and breathed into his nostrils the breath of life, and man became a living being (Gen. 2:4–7).

Harrell Beck points out that the document takes its name from the fact that the author uses the name *Jahweh* for God (translated "the Lord God" in the King James and the Revised Standard Version Bibles); and that the attempt to bring a mass of narratives, poems, and laws into some sort of a national epic was probably made in Hebron about 950–850 BCE.[28] The story of Jahwist tradition is set forth in the story of Abraham's call (Gen. 12:1–4); and Abraham is the hero. The main theme is that Jahweh is the God of Israel and Israel is his people.[29]

The Priestly account (Gen. 1–2:3) is said to be a later presentation begun by combining the Jahweist, Elohistic (in the North 750–700 BCE, whose hero was Moses), and the Deuteronomist documents (621 BCE) into what became known as a Priestly document about 550–400.[30] It is said to have been influenced by the teaching and preaching of Second Isaiah (Isa. 40–55) or Isaiah of the Exile, whose message was centred on God as the Creator of all things and God of all nations (Isa. 40:12–26, 41:18–20, 45:7). The experience of the Babylonian Exile brought new thoughts to Israel, and the priests had to recast their account concerning the creation story (Gen. 1–2:3). At the same time, issues of the origin and search for everlasting salvation became critical. The Priestly account gives a more detailed account on cosmological thinking from the beginning, not of time but of creation: "In the beginning God created the heavens and the earth. Now the earth was formless and empty, darkness was over the surface of the deep, and the Spirit of God was hovering over the waters" (Gen. 1:1–2).

What follows the creation of the heavens and the earth was called into existence by God: the light; an expanse (large open area); separation of the sea and the dry land; vegetation; the moon, stars; living creatures—livestock (Gen. 1:3–26). Finally, God created humankind, both male and female—and he blessed them, and urged them to multiply. "God saw all that he had made, and it was very good" (Gen. 1:31). Von Rad goes on to point out:

> The two presentations are alike in that they have as their chief end, though they do it in very different ways, the creation of man, that is, mankind as male and female—with the result that the rest of the world is ordered around them as the chief work of Jahweh in Creation, for Gen. 2:4bff too terminates and culminates in the creation of mankind represented in the duality of man and woman. Admittedly, in Gen. 2:4bff man is the mid-point around which God constructs his work, whereas in Gen. 1:1ff he is the apex of a cosmological pyramid. [Priestly] has a much greater interest in cosmological and in consequence he sketches a story of Creation which moves much more purposefully, though by stages, towards the creation of man.[31]

The Image of God in Humanity

From the Priestly account of the creation of humanity story, Jurgen Moltmann makes an interesting observation. He comments that after God had created the heavens and the earth, and called everything else into being by his creative word: "Let there be light . . . Let there be an expanse between waters to separate water from water . . . Let the land produce living creatures . . . ," when God came to the creation of humanity, he made a special resolve:[32]

> "Let us make mankind in our image, in our likeness, so that they may rule over the fish in the sea and the birds in the sky, over the livestock and all the wild animals, and over all the creatures that move along the ground." So God created mankind in his own image, in the image of

God he created them; male and female he created them. (Gen. 1:26–27)

One may raise the question, Why does God say, "Let us make mankind in our image, in our likeness?" Or why does he use the plural pronoun, "Let us . . ."? When I started studying theology, I thought Genesis 1:26–27 was the foundation for the Trinitarian doctrine, only to be corrected quickly that that was not the case. In the Shona culture of the people of Zimbabwe, like in other African ethnic groups, a plural pronoun is always used to address an elderly person, or persons who are respected. Similarly in the Hebrew, the plural form "*Elohim*, the generic (a kind, class, origin) term for God, denoting deity *par excellence*," because of its plural majesty is used, "let us make humankind in our image."[33]

First, the Jahwist account points out that on the same day that God created the earth and the heavens (Gen. 2:4b), he also formed man or the man; and the account does not speak of the formation of Adam.[34] "He is *adam*, 'man,' because he was formed from *adamah* 'ground' . . . and as such he is related to the animal kingdom, for later, 'out of the ground the Lord God formed every beast of the field and every bird of the air."[35]

The formation of man was not complete until the Lord God "breathed into his nostrils the breath of life, and the man became a living being" (Gen. 2:7). That means the human being created by God consisted of body and spirit—body, "from the dust of the ground," and spirit, "the breath of life" from the breath of God. Thus, we should not talk of a human being as *having* a body and spirit; rather, a human being *is* body and spirit. Migloire clearly points to the social dimension of the human being in the nature of his creation, "According to the biblical witness, human beings are created in the image of God not as solitary beings but in the duality of male and female."[36] Essentially, human beings are created not only as rational beings, but equally as social beings—male and female created for each other.

Second, humankind bears a "likeness" or resemblance of God, the Creator. The Psalmist puts it poetically and majestically when he praises God for his incomprehensible greatness: "When I consider your heavens, the work of your fingers, the moon and the stars, which you have set in place, what is mankind that you are mindful of them, human beings that you care for them?" (Ps. 8:3–4).

God is mindful of human beings because humanity was created in the image of God; and the question is, What is this image of God created in human beings? John Wesley's interpretation of Genesis 1:16–27 is as follows: (a) God created man "in his own natural image—a picture of his own immortality; endued with understanding, freedom of will and liberty."[37] (b) He created man in his political image—making man the governor of this lower world, having dominion over the fish, birds, and all creatures. (c) God created man in his own moral image[38]—meaning, righteousness and true holiness (Eph. 4:24),[39] or love. Man shared God's love for justice, mercy, and truth. This love was man's "sole principle of his tempers, thoughts, words and actions."[40] For Wesley, God's image in humanity is the natural image, political image, and the moral image.

For Daniel Migliore, (a) the image of God is not a physical resemblance of God for he forbids any kind of image of him; (b) the image of God resides in the capacity to reason; (c) humanity is given dominion over the earth; and (d) other interpreters emphasize the human freedom as the meaning of the image of God. However, in agreement with twentieth-century theologians, Migliore contends that "the symbol 'image of God' describes human life in relationship with God and with the other creatures."[41]

Moltmann makes another point about the image of God in humanity on earth: It is "the image of God" in humanity that causes the doctrines of the "immanence of God" and "providence of God" to make sense. He goes on to write: "This is apparent from the fact that God 'imprints' his image and his glory in his early creation, the human being, which means that he himself is drawn into the history of these creatures of his."[42]

Attributes of God

"The term 'attributes' of God means simply the adjectives that have been variously classified and listed by theologians in their attempts to speak meaningfully about God."[43] The word *attribute* means "to think of as belonging to or coming from a particular person or thing; assign or ascribe (to)."[44] The African people have several attributes they ascribe to God. Among the Shona people of Zimbabwe, these Godly characteristics include:

(1) *Just*, for he enables rain to fall, and the sun to shine on all people—the good and bad.

(2) *Merciful*, for he does not quickly react to humanity's wrongdoing, neither does he encourage the spirit of avenging.

(3) *Generous*, which is related to the Shona's anthropomorphic name for God—*pfuyavarombwo*—one who looks after the poor.

(4) *Holy*, and his holiness is manifested in some personalities who communicate with the ancestral spirits, and to God through such ancestors; as well as to places of worship in the mountains, and some big trees, to mention a few.

Christian theology echoes a few of these attributes of God in both the Old and New Testaments:

(1) *Holiness.* What do we mean when we say God is holy? Isaiah exclaimed, "Holy, holy, holy is the Lord Almighty; the whole earth is full of his glory" (Isa. 6:3). The New Testament Greek word is *hagiasmos*, translated *holiness* in English (Rom. 6:19, 22). Essentially, it means "what is separated from ordinary or profane [secular] is holy."[45] Walter Klaiber says, "Whoever talks about holiness has to talk about God: about encountering God (Exod. 3:5), about nearness to God (Isa. 6:3), about fellowship with God,"[46] for God alone is holy, and holiness belongs to

him alone. "But God is holy in as much as God is 'wholly Other,' who is inaccessible, incomprehensible, and unattainable to humankind."[47]

God's "holiness extends to human beings: e.g. priests or pastors, equipment use in temple or church, festivals celebrated (Lev. 23) . . . In the NT . . . Jesus is holy (Luke 1:35), the church too is holy indwelt by the Holy Spirit, any behaviour which violates this relationship is reprehensible (Rom. 5:5, 2 Cor. 6:16–7:1)."[48] Similarly, all who have been baptized in the name of the Father, the Son, and the Holy Spirit become a holy people—"a holy priesthood," Peter wrote (1 Pet. 2:5). "The term [holy or holiness] indicated a relationship more than quality."[49] It is in such a relationship that God imparts his holiness as a gift, and growing out of justification or God's activity for and within us by faith.

The African people talk of holy mountains and other holy places. These places are set aside for worship of the Creator through the ancestral spirits. And that holiness extends to leaders of this traditional worship.

(2) *Righteousness.* What is righteousness? What do we mean when we say God is righteous? "Abram believed the Lord, and he credited it to him as righteousness" (Gen. 15:6). The New Testament word is *dikaiosune*, meaning righteousness. It

> is the character or quality of being right or just; it was formerly spelled '*rightwiseness*' which clearly expresses the meaning. It is used to denote an attribute of God, e.g. Rom. 3:5, the context of which shows that 'the righteousness of God' means essentially the same as his faithfulness, or truthfulness, that which is consistent with his own nature and promises; Rom. 3:25, 26 speaks of his righteousness as exhibited in the death of Christ, which is sufficient to show men that God is neither indifferent to sin nor regards it lightly.[50]

"While the righteousness of God is very closely related to holiness as conceived in Jewish and Christian thought, it is sufficiently distinct to merit brief separate discussion."[51] "There is absolutely no concept in the Old Testament with so central significance for all the relationships of human life as that of righteousness . . . It is the standard not only for man's relationship to God, but also for his relationships to his fellows, reaching down . . . to animals and his natural environment."[52]

(3) *The Absolute Being of God*. "By 'absolute being' is here meant being free from dependence upon or limitation by any other being. Instead of 'absolute being' we might use the phrase 'independent existence.'"[53] The following attributes are given concerning this absolute being of God:

(a) *The Omnipresence of God*. In the Old Testament, God is Yahweh "enthroned in Zion" (Ps. 9:11), and Mount Zion is where he dwells (Ps. 74:2). In the New Testament, "God is Spirit" (John 4:24) and he is everywhere. He is no longer a spatial being, limited by space. Instead he is all-embracing of all events and creation. Hence, Paul says to the Athenians, "For in him we live and move and have our being" (Acts 17:28).

(b) *The Omnipotence of God*. The Hebrews described God as *El Shaddai*, meaning "The Almighty." As it appears in the New Testament, this power is for the sake of his children to be victorious (John 17:15, Luke 24:6, Acts 1:8, 2:4).

(c) *The Omniscience of God*. "If God can do all that can be done He can know all that can be known. If He can control all things according to His purpose, so far as He wills to control them, He must know all things so far as He wills to know them . . . . God, however, must be limited by his own nature and purpose. For example, if He has put a check on His power to give man freedom of will, then He must have limited somewhat His knowledge of the future . . ."[54] (This is similar to the experience of a parent of a son or daughter who is eighteen years of age or older.)

(d) *Transcendence and Immanence of God*. "The doctrine of transcendence seems to need the tension or balance provided by the doctrine of immanence."[55]

(i) The idea of transcendence comes from the thinking that God should not be identified with anything on this earth. This is true, even in African mythology. He is high and lifted up. God is considered to transcend the world because he is more than his creation, he is other than us, and he is other than the Material Universe.[56]

(ii) *The Immanence of God.* The doctrine of immanence provides the tension that God is also immanent in us and in our world. This is affirmed in a number of ways: He now sustains us. "Even though I walk through the valley of the shadow of death, I will fear no evil . . . (Ps. 23:4); "So do not fear, for I am with you . . ." (Isa. 41:10); "Give us today our daily bread" (Matt. 6:12); "Look at the birds of the air . . ." (Matt. 6:26). The African prayer vividly expresses the concept of the immanence of God: "Walk in front of me; walk behind me; and walk beside me." And, he knows our very thoughts.[57]

(4) *Love of God.* "The supreme righteousness known to the Christian community is love."[58] The prophet Hosea took an adulterous woman, Homer, into marriage to demonstrate God's love for the rebellious Israel (Hos. 1:2). There are three types of love: (a) *Eros* is self-satisfied love or self-centred love. It loves someone not because of the person or his or her condition, but for itself—for what it gets out of the person. (b) *Philos*—friend, but "primarily an adjective, denoting love, dear, or friendly."[59] Thus, *philos* means friendly love, or love for a friend. (c) *Agape* means primarily Christian love.—loving a person for what he or she is, and would become (John 21:15–17).

Chapter 4

Humanity and Sin

When I was a young person growing up in rural Africa, each time I saw a chameleon, I made a point to stone it to death. The reason for that unfortunate behaviour was a folktale that had been shared with me by my elders. The folktale went like this: Once upon a time God urgently wanted a message delivered to his people, so he asked the chameleon to deliver the message. The message was that when people die, they will have a second chance to come back and live again.

The chameleon, with his slow style of walking, took his time responding. God got tired of waiting for a response from the chameleon, so he also sent the lizard, who moves fast. This time the message had changed. It was that when people die, they die for good, and there was no second chance. The lizard responded so quickly that he overtook the chameleon on the way, and delivered the difficult message to the people before him. A few days later, the chameleon arrived and delivered his good-news message to the people. Even though the chameleon had a message that people much preferred, because they had already received the lizard's message, they would not accept the chameleon's message. The people took the chameleon to be a false messenger, and they stoned him to death.

As young people, my friends and I also expressed our anger toward the chameleon for not getting to the people fast enough with the message from God that was more favourable for humanity. We felt the chameleon had done humanity wrong. The chameleon deserved to be punished for its wrongdoing or sin, so we stoned every chameleon we saw. Its sin was the failure to deliver the message from God quickly enough or earlier than the lizard.

African Concept of Sin

First, we will look at African mythology and the fall of humanity. The concept of falling from God's favour and the subsequent estrangement between God and humanity expresses a great truth about the complexity of human life. It is often said that the greatest sin of humanity is to fall out of God's favour—distancing us from God, our fellow humans, and the rest of creation. Several African ethnic groups, even long before the advent of Christianity, taught the doctrine of falling from the favour of God. The following are some of the mythical stories that share how humanity fell from God's favour, and thereafter experienced an estranged relationship with him.

From West Africa we learn the following teaching:

> God once dwelt close to or on earth (for heaven was near then) until an accidental offense against him (or actual disobedience, usually by a woman wanting more or better food) compelled God to remove the heaven far away and to break his direct link with humanity. The Ashanti (southern Ghana) say God, *Nyame* (also known as *Onyakopon*), withdrew heaven from the earth because he was annoyed when the low floor of heaven was knocked from below by the pestle of an old woman who was pounding *fufu* (mashed yams). So he climbed up to heaven on a thread, like a great Spider (*Ananse Kokroko*) that he is. Mischievous still, the old woman ordered her children to build a tower of mortars, one on top of another, right to the sky. Nearing one more mortar, the children took it from the bottom—and the whole edifice collapsed, killing many.[1]

Similarly, the *Dinka* people of southern Sudan have a myth that teaches:

> There used to be a rope that hung down from heaven, and people could climb it when they wished to speak to God. When the woman kept hitting the underside of heaven with her pestle, God withdrew the heavens and he had the rope withdrawn.[2]

The Shona people of Zimbabwe teach that originally God lived among the people, but removed himself to heaven because people bothered him with questions they had answers for, and things that they could do for themselves. After God removed himself from the people, there existed estrangement between God and humanity. Though the people tried to reestablish the previous glorious relationship that was lost, not only between God and humanity, but also among the various ethnic groups of humanity, it all proved vanity.

What the above mythical stories teach us is that the cause for God to withdraw his close relationship with humanity was humanity itself.

Second, a deeper examination of the African concept of sin is in order. Africans do not often conceptualize the issue of sin as an idea or an abstraction. Instead, sin is often attached to a person—the sinner. Thus, instead of asking, what is sin?, one would ask, who is a sinner? Or, who is considered a traitor to the family, clan, or community? For Africans, sin is often understood as violating the second commandment: "Love your neighbor as yourself" (Mark 12:31). In fact, to sin against God is understood as sinning against humanity or a neighbour. Thus, sin is identified with evil forces and human acts as they are experienced within the family, the clan, and community relationships.

Laurenti Magesa has identified what he calls "the Enemies of Life" in conjunction with life in Africa as "wrongdoings (wrong actions), illness, and witchcraft."[3] In Africa, illness and witchcraft belong together because they all lead to death. Therefore, a person who is known or more often suspected to be a witch is the most feared and hated person in the community. In some areas, if a family suspects their neighbour is a witch, they may even move to a new neighbourhood. Such suspected witches then are isolated as other people also move away from them.

Another unwanted enemy of society is a murderer—one who might have killed a spouse or neighbour or a stranger for reasons he/she alone knows. In olden days, in some communities of the Shona culture of the people of Zimbabwe, a person who was known by the extended family and community to have been a *maroyi* (practitioner of witchcraft) or a murderer, at his or her death was not buried at the family or village cemetery. Rather, he or she was buried at a separate place. Families and communities took this kind of action to detach themselves from sinful actions of the deceased, and also to teach the seriousness of failing to live harmoniously with others in the community.

Such separation of an individual from the family or communal cemetery also presupposed a rejection of the individual by the ancestral community—the community in the next life. It also was believed that the spirits of persons rejected by the ancestors in the next world come back as wandering spirits among the living. They are often known for coming back as spooks or demons—living in trees, and anywhere they find space.

Christian Teaching on Sin

First, let us look at the fall of humanity in the Bible. In the Garden of Eden, there were two commands—to work and to take care of the Garden (Gen. 2:15). Work was and to this day is not a curse. Rather, work is a privilege and a blessing to participate in God's vineyard or the new creation of God. Among trees in the Garden of Eden, two were mentioned specifically. There was "the tree of life" (Gen. 2:9), which represented the giving of life, without death, to those who eat its fruit (Gen. 3:22, Rev. 2:7, 22:2, 14).[4] There was also "the tree of the knowledge of good and evil" (Gen. 2:9). Adam and Eve had the freedom to do everything and anything except to eat of that one forbidden tree (Gen. 2:17). The tree represented or signified "giving knowledge of good and evil, leading ultimately to death to those who eat its fruit" (Gen. 2:17, 3:3). "Knowledge of good and evil" refers to moral knowledge or ethical discernment (Deut. 1:39, Isa. 7:15–16)."[5] Or, as Charles Kraft points out, the symbolism of the knowledge of good and evil (Gen. 2:17) represented "total wisdom, God-like omniscience (see 2 Sam. 14:17, Isa. 7:15–16). Therefore, the tree was strictly forbidden. Adam and Eve were presented with the choice to obey God's command or to disobey.[6] That means:

> Adam and Eve possessed both life and moral discernment as they came from the hand of God. Their access to the tree of life showed that God's will and intention for them was life. Ancient pagans believed that the gods intended for man always to be mortal. In eating the fruit of the tree of the knowledge of good and evil, Adam and Eve sought a creaturely source of discernment in order to be morally independent of God.[7]

Second, we will explore the nature of sin. The serpent's persuasion of Eve led both Eve and Adam to eat the fruit of the forbidden tree (Gen. 3:6). Thus, by choosing to disobey God in eating the fruit of knowledge and evil, instead of the fruit of the tree of life, Adam and Eve sinned against God. That sin of disobedience to God is the sin of all humanity to this day.

In teaching about the fall of humanity, John Wesley points out that Adam and Eve disobeyed God by eating the fruit of a forbidden tree. That wilful act of disobedience to their Creator showed that Adam and Eve had openly declared that they would no longer have God to rule over them.[8] Thus, they "lost the knowledge and the love of God, without which the image of God could not subsist [to continue to be in use]."[9] Thus, humanity died to God—"the most dreadful of all deaths."[10] Adam and Eve's fall was the fall of humanity everywhere and for all time. Because of that fall, humans became deprived, unholy, unhappy, sank into pride and self will, the very image of the devil, and turned themselves to sensual appetites and desires, which is the image of the beasts that perish.[11]

John Wesley went on to say that humanity related to God is *spiritual*, but when turned away from God, humanity becomes *fleshy* and its whole nature is twisted.[12] Wesley also said, "Man was created looking directly to God, as his last end; but, falling into sin, he fell off from God, and turned into himself."[13] In this state, all humanity is like the rebellious nation of Israel, and has become sick. He continued:

> The whole head is sick, and the whole heart faint . . . (Isa. 1:5, KJV) . . . From the sole of the foot even unto the head there is no soundness; but wounds, and bruises, and petrifying sores . . . From all these we learn, concerning man in his natural state, unassisted by the grace of God, that "every imagination of the thoughts of his heart is" still "evil, only evil," and that "continually" (Gen. 6:5) . . . there is no one righteous, not even one; there is no one who understands, no one who seeks God. All have turned away, they have together become worthless; there is no one who does good, not even one. (Rom. 3:10–12)[14]

Although John Wesley took the Genesis account of the Garden of Eden and the fall of Adam very seriously, he also believed that "the present account of man is confirmed by daily experience."[15] Humanity continues to disobey God to this day.

Third, let us review some definitions of sin. Christian tradition often made a distinction between actual sin and original sin. We shall look at definitions that have been shared by various theologians in relation to actual sin.

(a) "In both Roman Catholic and Protestant orthodox traditions, actual sin is defined as any act, which includes thoughts as well as deeds, done in conscious and deliberate violation of God's will as expressed in the revealed or natural law."[16]

(b) For Augustine of Hippo, *pride* is the beginning of all sin. Pride is when the soul craves to desert its Creator as its source of life, so as to make itself as if it were its own source. "This happens when the soul loves itself too much; when it abandons that immutable good, which it ought to love more than itself. This falling away was voluntary, since if the will had remained steadfast in its love of that higher immutable good which gave it light to see it and warmth to love it, it would not have turned away to self-satisfaction . . ."[17]

(c) "Sin is man's failure to be what he was created to be."[18] For example, Israel failed to be true to the covenant of God, and the prodigal son became rebellious to his loving father. At times it helps to acknowledge that some of us today live in poverty when we should be living in abundant life.

(d) Daniel Migliore says, "The origin and nature of sin cannot be adequately depicted without recourse to paradoxical statements. Among the most important of these paradoxes are the following: (i) Sin is a *universal condition*, but it is also a *self-chosen act* for which we are responsible . . . (ii) Sin insinuates itself into all human action, including not only what is widely condemned as *evil* but also what is commonly praised as *good*. (iii) Sin is a corruption of the *individual* person, but it is also active and powerful in public and *corporate* structures.[19]

(e) The Bible uses many words to describe sin. There are terms in the Old Testament such as *missing the mark, distortion of what is right, rebellion against a superior, unfaithfulness to a covenant, folly* (foolish action or belief), and *senselessness* (not showing good sense, stupid). The most common New Testament terms for sin are: *missing the mark, transgression of the law, trespass,* and *unrighteousness.*[20]

(f) Therefore, according to the Genesis story of the fall of mankind, sin is *disobedience* to God; it is sinning against God. Sin is also sinning against another person; thus sin is personal and corporate.[21]

(g) Sin is *deviation* from the right way; that is, "to miss a goal or way; e.g. among the Benjamite warriors there were men who could sling stones at an hair-breath, and not miss"[22] or "each of who could sling a stone at a hair and not miss" (Judg. 20:16). Thus, sin is failing to do something in relation to man or God. The same idea underlies words such as *iniquity, err,* and *wickedness.* Under the idea of deviation is also the word *perversity,* which means deviation, distortion, and crookedness of what is properly upright. It is a conscious, arrogant attitude that inevitably leads to strife and disharmony.[23]

(h) Sin is *rebellion against a superior or unfaithfulness.* The Hebrew word *pasha,* inadequately translated "trespass" and "transgression," views sin as rebellion against God.[24]

(i) "Sin also means that the soul itself is diseased, to a degree determined by the consideration: did the action arise in the centre of the will, or did it merely lie on the circumstances?"[25]

Fourth, we will look at original sin. Harvey said that in the classical Christian tradition, "original sin refers to the universal and hereditary sinfulness of man since the fall of Adam. It is contrasted with actual sin, which is a self-conscious violation of God's law."[26] Although some of the earliest church theologians, such as Justin Martyr (100–225 CE), Irenaeus (130–200 CE), Tertullian (150–225 CE), and Origen (185–254 CE) might have been aware of the idea of this universal sinfulness of humanity as inherited, it was Augustine (354–430 CE) who formulated the doctrine and connected it with Adam's sin.[27]

> Once having fallen, therefore, man cannot by his own efforts regain his former status in being. This is expressed in Augustine's notion that before the fall angels and men possessed the ability not to sin . . . as well as the ability to sin . . . but that after the fall they possessed only the latter. Adam's sin, then, has corrupted the entire human race and it is a mass of sin . . . and justly subject to damnation. By this Augustine means not only that man inherits a tendency to sin but that he inherits guilt.[28]

Augustine called this strong or abnormal desire to sin *concupiscence*, a condition only overcome by baptism.

If one agrees with Migliore that "the symbol 'image of God' describes human life in relationship with God and with the other creatures"[29] and the dictum that the fall of Adam is the experience of humanity everywhere and every time, then one may not have to be concerned with the issue of sin or original sin as inheritance from another person. It remains clear that both actual sin and original sin are traceable to how the individual, family, corporate, community, or nation uses its capacity to reason and will to choose.

Chapter 5

Evil and the Providence of God

In some circles evil and the providence of God is known as *theodicy*—a term derived from the Greek words literally meaning "deity" and "justice." As the word has been used, it means theological attempt to justify faith in God's goodness in spite of the abundant evidence of evil in the world. In ordinary use the term has often come to refer to theological affirmations about the problem of evil.[1]

In the Shona language, when a person describes a so-called evil person one may say, "U*ne mwoyo wakaipa*," meaning he/she has a bad heart, and that he/she is always thinking of doing bad and harmful things to others. Or, a person may say, "U*ne mwoyo mukukutu*," meaning he/she has a hard heart; he/she is never merciful to anyone. At times when one describes a difficult situation where one does not seem to see a solution, one says, "*Zvaita mai watsva kumusana, mwana achitsva dumbu*." This refers to Shona women's cultural and traditional way of carrying a baby on their backs. Literally it means if a mother's back is burned, and a child's tummy is also burned, there is no way she can carry the baby as usual. It simply means the situation in which an individual finds himself or herself is difficult with no way out.

There are several evil things that can happen to an individual or family that lead a person to use the above saying. Perhaps a parent who was the breadwinner dies; at the same time a child is admitted at a university where fees are expected to be paid. It is such a challenge where one expresses one's predicament: "*Zvaita mai watsva kumusana, mwana achitsva dumbu*." The force of evil is felt not only in individuals, but also in families, communities, and nations.

Defining Evil

Imagine on a rainy day a family consisting of a husband, wife, and four children sitting around the fire in their nice grass thatched kitchen. All of a sudden lightning strikes the kitchen, killing everybody except the youngest child who is less than a year old. This child is thrown outside the kitchen by the impact of the lightning and as the house catches fire. Or, imagine a good number of innocent young women and girls abducted by a military tangent to be used as sex slaves, and no one raises a finger to defend the rights of these women. Would you not be tempted to ask, Where is God in all this? If so, we may begin to understand the prophet Habakkuk when he cried out:

> How long, Lord, must I call for help, but you do not listen? Or cry out to you, "Violence!" but you do not save? Why do you make me look at injustice? Why do you tolerate wrongdoing? Destruction and violence are before me; there is strife, and conflict abounds. Therefore the law is paralyzed, and justice never prevails. The wicked hem in the righteous, so that justice is perverted. (Hab. 1:1–4)

According to the *Webster's New World Dictionary*, evil means "morally bad or wrong, wicked, depraved; causing pain or trouble; harmful; injurious."[2] Evil is a bad situation, often involving pain, suffering, even death. Evil is also "attributed to disobedience to God's will or to natural calamities."[3] Evil causes misunderstanding and disunity to a people—families, churches, and communities.

Often the Old Testament viewed evil calamities or disasters brought to Israel as punishment by God (Jer. 26:19, Amos 3:6); and God is viewed as responsible for both good and evil (Ps. 78:49). Some people, including some Christians in Africa, held a similar view when HIV and AIDS initially hit their countries. They thought God was punishing those people infected for their wrongdoing. To a moralist, that argument may sound plausible, but why should an innocent spouse infected by a husband or wife also suffer? The problem in all this has been an attempt to pinpoint the wrongdoing. Despite that God created the world and declared everything in it good (Gen. 1:10), every generation of humanity has constantly raised some questions about the problem of evil: Why is this world so evil? Why does God allow evil? Why does he allow such calamities? Are the universe, the nation, or families in which we live still friendly? Do we survive by good luck or should we believe in what we are taught as God's providence? All these questions cover both natural and moral evil.

Each time we pick up a national newspaper, we are appalled by reports of corruption, theft, rape, murder, or genocide, and many other horrendous things happening around us. The cases of murder and abuse of innocent children by adults to satisfy traditional rites has become an issue of great concern in the whole region of sub-Saharan Africa. The desire to get rich by whatever means at the expense of everyone else has become a corruptive practice by both the humble and respected citizenry of all nations. Unfortunately, the more one tries to correct oneself the more one continues to sink in one's sinfulness.

Problems and disasters do come, even in Christian families. It could be terminal illness or a sudden death of a family member. Relatives or family members may react differently to such problems. Some Christians meet troubles of illness with passive resignation to the will of God. They may entertain a sense of hope, that somehow things will work out. At the same time, some Christians would interpret the doctrine of providence "as a kind of an insurance against evil, thinking that it cannot touch the believer."[4] One often hears preachers say that if you have faith in God, these evil things will not happen to you. Or if you accept Jesus Christ, he will protect you from all forces of evil. The problem is that if and when trouble does come, such Christians think that God has deceived them. Standing against this teaching is the biblical view "that evil, and the suffering to which it leads, is real; but that it is within the Providence of God and can be overcome."[5] Further questions could be raised: Why does God seem to tolerate evil? Does he really care? What is the source of these evil forces?

Source of Evil

The source of evil is apparently intricately interwoven with the good things God has created and granted to humanity for its welfare. In "The Parable of the Weeds" Jesus is not dealing so much with the source of evil as he is affirming the point that "the people of the kingdom live side by side with the people of the evil one."[6] That is a reality of life. We shall take a look at what seems to be two sources of evil—natural evil and moral evil.

First, *natural evil*. Humanity lives in the world of nature, and there are calamities such as floods, earthquakes, fires, and droughts that humanity may not have control over. Time and again, human beings suffer immensely at the hands of nature. Despite all its beauty, wealth, and economic advantages, nature also produces calamities that cause humanity to suffer. Who can forget the 2004 tsunami that hit Indonesia and other countries that border the Indian Ocean, the earthquake that struck Japan in 2011, the great wildfires that burned across California in 2015 and 2016, a series of droughts that have plagued African countries, floods—causing a woman in Mozambique to give birth to a child up in a tree, and many others? These natural calamities have caused immense loss of life and property and left thousands of people with deep emotional and physical pain and suffering. People continue asking, Why does God allow such things to happen?

In spite of all the loss and pain that humanity suffers from these natural calamities, Marcus Ward points out that "were God to make the floods impossible, He would make impossible also the growth of food."[7] For example, consider the millions of people who benefit from floods that occur in some of our big rivers, depositing alluvial soul on and over their banks, without which there would be no agricultural activities.

Second, *moral evil*. Moral evil is "the suffering and evil that sinful human beings inflict on each other and on the world they inhabit."[8] God's gift to humanity—freedom—opens the door to the possibility of sin.[9] Freedom means that an individual may choose the wrong or right option. God took this risk when he chose to make human beings free. "He did not will evil, but He willed a state of affairs in which evil is possible."[10] In olden times, parents in most countries prearranged marriages for their sons and daughters. Today the freedom to choose one's spouse is increasingly in the hands of those who wish to marry. Some people cite abuse of this freedom for young people to choose as a reason for the high rate of divorce today. But the intention was for the young people to freely make their choice. The principle was just and fair.

It was noble to achieve political freedom and independence for many young nations that were under the thumb of colonial powers. Unfortunately, there are leaders who have used those noble intentions to consolidate power and wealth for themselves, forgetting their people. Opportunities to democratize systems and institutions that lead toward good governance became paralyzed. For many people in such countries, poverty seems to be growing worse. Indeed, many are denied freedom of association, freedom of movement, and freedom of speech, as well as other human rights.

In relation to moral evil, Marcus Ward also talks of the suffering we go through because we live in solidarity with others. For instance, there is "the suffering that we have to endure but which cannot be traced to our own sinning."[11] God has made the world or universe so that life lived in solidarity with others is the basis for both good and evil. We live in accord as nations, communities, and families. If the head of this group is good, all live to benefit; if he or she is evil, all suffer. It is painful to see a man or woman dismissed from work because of misconduct—causing the whole family to suffer because of his/her dismissal. Even innocent children suffer because of misconduct that they were no part of. Again, a government may pass through Parliament policies that create divisions in a nation, a decline of the economy, unemployment, and all kinds of suffering to its citizens due to our life in solidarity with each other. That means all have to suffer because they live in solidarity as a nation.

Overcoming moral evil may require men and women of courage to sacrifice even their own lives in order to find the way forward. Ward has suggested (a) that the love of God "which make the existence of evil a problem for the believer, is also its solution."[12] He quotes T. E. Jessop, who in his writings on *Nature, History and God* concluded by saying, "Love is the only good thing that can be trusted to bring forth what looks like evil and handle it safely."[13] Ward also suggests that (b) "To stress that so many people accept suffering bravely . . . [He went on to say] nothing can be made of man till he learns courage and this is learned only in danger and difficulty."[14] Jesus showed the way through dying for humanity (John 3:16). There also are those who have demonstrated courageous life and leadership in our history: Mahatma Ghandi of India, Martin Luther King Jr. of America, and Nelson Mandela of South Africa, to name a few.

Satan or the Devil

We continue to ask why evil has entered the world that God made good. Specifically, why did God allow Satan in the world? This "requires us to consider what is involved in the idea of personal power of evil usually named Satan or the Devil, i.e., the Prince rather than merely the principle of evil."[15]

Who is this strong and influential character known as Satan? I recall an incident where a certain man who had been involved in a most degrading and shameful behaviour was brought before a village court. Village courts among the Shona people of Zimbabwe are open and democratic, as they allow every member of the village to attend—men, women, children, and strangers. I do not remember if the man was Christian or not.

However, when he was asked, Why did you do it? the man pleaded guilty and asked for forgiveness because at the time he committed the offence, he said, "I was not myself. Satan had entered into me." Humanity's game with evil is always to blame others for one's failures. Adam blamed Eve, Eve blamed the serpent, and so the man blamed Satan.

First, the name "Satan" is derived from a Hebrew root word that primarily means to obstruct or oppose.[16] In the Old Testament, the name is used in three passages (all post-exilic) to refer to a supernatural being (Job 1–2, Zech. 3:1–2) (519 BCE), and when Satan influenced David (1 Chron. 21:1). We also note that in the Old Testament the devil is mentioned as malignant [having an evil influence] spirits or demons (Deut. 32:17, Ps. 106:37); and in later Judaism, the idea is developed and expounded (Gen. 6:1–5, Isa. 14:12) to show that existence of the evil spirits is due not to God's creation but to the rebellion of free spirits against God. Satan appears as the head of the hierarchy of evil powers, and is known by several names: *Beliar*, *Beelzebul*, *Azazel*, and is said to be an angel, originally good but now fallen (2 Enoch 29:4).[17] Francis Beare says that some of the names mentioned above, including *Asmodeus*, *Beliar* and *Beelzebul*, were given to Satan in later Jewish and Christian writings.[18] Thus because Satan is a fallen figure, he is the enemy of human beings and seeks to destroy them by attacking the body with disease and the soul with temptation. He was identified with the serpent in Gen. 3, and made responsible for sin and death (Ws 2:24).[19]

In the New Testament the name Satan appears thirty-three times, and also thirty-two times as *diabolos* in Greek, meaning the Devil. He is also known by several other names: "the tempter" (Matt. 4:3), "the evil one" (Matt. 13:19), "the accuser" (Rev. 12:10), "the enemy" (Matt. 13:39), "the devil," "the prince of demons" (Matt. 9:34), and "the ruler of the world" (John 12:31). He also bears the name *Beliar* (2 Cor. 6:15), and Jesus calls him *Beelzebul* (Matt. 10:25). In the New Testament, Satan is represented as a distinct personality who enters into human beings and becomes the author of evil deeds and passions.[20] The Jewish doctrine of a personal devil is prominent in the New Testament, which thinks in general of evil as the Evil One (Matt. 4:1, Mark 1:12, Luke 4:1, John 8:44, 1 Cor. 5:5, 1 Pet. 5:8, Rev. 12:7–17). This is the way New Testament Christians explained the origin and problem of evil in the world. It is essential to note that the name Satan or Devil "may still be used to symbolize everything that is against the will of God and so for the believer, the enemy."[21]

There is no doubt that the early Christians, like most of the Jews of their time, believed that there was a strong spirit of evil called Satan or the Devil. Francis Beare says, "None the less, we must recognize that this is a mythical conception that has lost appeal to the minds of men; we cannot ourselves accept it without falling victims to superstition."[22]

Talking of mythical conception is not new to the African people. African folktales are full of mythical conceptions. Among the Shona folktales, there is no cleverer animal than the rabbit. In all stories involving the rabbit and the lion, the rabbit and the hyena, the rabbit and fox, the rabbit always wins the day. Not only was the rabbit clever, he also was a cheater.

For example, it is told that one day the rabbit and the hyena, who were still bachelors, agreed that they did not need their mothers anymore, for soon they were going to be married and their wives would take care of all their needs. They plotted to kill their mothers, although they were still providing food for them. The hyena executed the agreement that evening; he killed his mother. The rabbit relocated his mother to a hidden place, and from time to time the rabbit still enjoyed meals prepared by his mother. The hyena's health began deteriorating for lack of good food, and he began wondering why his friend's health remained steady. One day, after the hyena and the rabbit had had a good day together, and parted for their different homes, the hyena decided to secretly follow the rabbit to his home. The hyena then discovered the rabbit still had his mother. The following day, when the rabbit got to the place where they always met at a regular time, the hyena did not show up. Instead the hyena went to the new residence of the rabbit, and he killed and ate the rabbit's mother, for he was very hungry.

This is a mythical story with profound truth about human relationships, and that is why African ancestors shared such stories with young people. In their time, such stories communicated the truth of community life. There are people who are like the rabbit, cheating and grabbing all they can from their neighbours. They are cunning characters—evil ones—and they are like Satan. The main thing to remember is that our ancestors were able to communicate effectively even to our present generation the truth about the evil nature of such characters through the story of a rabbit and a hyena. Yet, who has ever seen a rabbit and a hyena talk? Such is the role of mythical conception in the African community.

When it comes to identifying the locus of moral evil, James, the brother of Jesus, the leader of the Jerusalem Council (Acts 15), martyred around 62 CE, shared a precise theological insight, showing his readers that Satan's locus is bundled in human desires and appetites:

> When tempted, no one should say, "God is tempting me." For God cannot be tempted by evil, nor does he tempt anyone; but each person is tempted when they are dragged away by their own evil desire and enticed. Then, after desire has conceived, it gives birth to sin; and sin, when it is full-grown, gives birth to death. (James 1:13–15)

Looking back into the history of the Hebrews or Jews, from the time of Abraham (2166 BCE), we find that Old Testament theology does not seem to have problems with Satan. The Jews were aware of Abraham's call by God (Gen. 12:1ff) and God's covenants with him (Gen. 15:1ff,

17:1ff) in which God claimed the Hebrews to be his people. At Mount Sinai, Moses received an outgrowth and extension of the Lord's covenant with Abraham and his descendants; and participation in divine blessings was conditioned on obedience added to faith (Gen. 17:9):

> You yourselves have seen what I did to Egypt, and how I carried you on eagles' wings and brought you to myself. Now if you obey me fully and keep my covenant, then out of all nations you will be my treasured possession. Although the whole earth is mine, you will be for me a kingdom of priests and a holy nation. (Exod. 19:4–6)

All along the history of the Hebrews, *their challenge was to keep God's covenant*. We have examples where the Hebrews faced failure, and no word of Satan is mentioned. First, Moses is barred from entering into the Promised Land. He struck the stone twice (Num. 20:9–12), and Moses died on Mount Nebo (Deut. 32:48ff).

Second, Achan and his family and property were stoned and burned in the valley of Achor, again because of disobedience to God's command (Josh. 7:19ff).

Third, Samson's downfall was due to revealing to Delilah the secret of his strength when he said, "No razor has ever been used on my head" (Judg. 16:17).

Fourth, David and Bathsheba, who David was enticed by as he watched her bathe (2 Sam. 11:1ff). David sees his sinfulness after being rebuked by Nathan (2 Sam 12:1ff, Ps. 32). Fifth, the prophet Jeremiah (22:1ff) passes judgment against the evil kings of Judah for policies that led the nation into exile.

Old Testament theology perceives sin in the individual, in families, in nations, in corporations, and in governments. There is no blaming of Satan, and the only solution is confession before the Lord.

The Providence of God

The word *providence* comes from two Latin words *pro*, meaning before, and *videre*, to see. It means "to see before," which is "fore ordering" or "seeing to it."[23] The idea of providence is said to have begun with the Stoics, the ancient Greek philosophers, who emerged at the beginning of the fourth century and who taught that "man has no free-will, but acts as does the rest of the universe, by the force of necessary laws . . ."[24] or "that the way things happened was inevitable but still good."[25] Christians understand the idea of the providence of God to mean:

> (1) Preservation as God's purpose for his creation (man and the world). Some Christians wanted to point to a certain event and say that it was God's purpose. However, preservation really means that despite what happens, God has a good purpose. (2) In popular thought God was thought of as a king, leading to the idea of Him as Governor. (3) Divine cooperation means that God and man work together in making things happen. John Calvin believed that God's providence meant God knew and decided in advance what would happen. John Wesley disagreed; what God knows is that men will act with freedom, he said.[26]

Another definition says providence is:

> the belief that over all the vicissitudes [condition of constant change or unpredictable changes] of humankind and the evolution of the universe there is a conscious purpose of God for good. There is a reason, however opaque [not letting light through], for everything. God is responsible not only for making but also for preserving the created order, and history is a process moving ever onwards

> towards an end, which God foresees (Ps. 104:31–35). In the NT the providence of God is demonstrated above all in Jesus, who is the guarantor that promises of God from of old are being fulfilled and will lead to salvation for mankind (1 Pet. 1:3–9).[27]

Paul lifts up the message of God's providence to all humanity when he says to the Gentiles in Lystra:

> In the past he let all nations go their own way. Yet he has not left himself without testimony. He has shown kindness by giving you rain from heaven and crops in their seasons; he provides you with plenty of food and fills your hearts with joy. (Acts 14:16–17)

Thus, the providence of God refers to the lordship of God—the providential care of God of the whole world. A song such as "He has the whole-wide world in his hand" expresses the profundity of the idea of God's providence. The Psalmist caught this mood when he sang, "Even though I walk through the valley of the shadow of death, I will fear no evil, for you are with me; your rod [instrument of authority as in Ps. 2:9—used also by shepherds in counting, guiding, rescuing and protecting sheep] and your staff [instrument of support] they comfort me" (Ps. 23:4). Migliore says, "The true God is no absentee landlord but remains faithful, upholding, blessing, and guiding the creation to its appointed goal. God's continuing care for all creatures is asserted in many passages of Scripture (e.g. Ps. 104:27–30), perhaps the most familiar being Matt. 5:45, 6:26–30, 10:30."[28]

One of the most fascinating stories in the Bible that demonstrates the providence of God is the story of Joseph. He became a victim of his father's favouritism to him over his brothers; he also became a young man of dreams—a thing that was not appreciated by the brothers. In return, the brothers who hated him sold him to the Midianite merchants who then sold him to Potiphar, a top official of Pharaoh in Egypt. By resisting the temptation to lie with Potiphar's wife, Joseph ended up in prison. Joseph was not only a young man of dreams, he also had the ability to interpret dreams of others. After interpreting Pharaoh's dreams Joseph was elevated to a high position, second only to Pharaoh over the land of Egypt. Through Joseph's obedient commitment to his God, Jacob and his family, as well as the people of Egypt and surrounding countries, survived the disastrous famine in and around Egypt.

Chapter 6

Christology

As Jesus and his disciples went to the villages around Caesarea Philippi, he asked his disciples, "Who do people say I am?"

"Some say John the Baptist; others say Elijah; and still others, one of the prophets," they replied.

"But what about you?" he asked. "Who do you say I am?"

Peter answered, "You are the Christ" (Mark 8:27–29). Jesus was reluctant to use the title "Christ." Whenever he used the term, he tried to use it not for himself (12:35, 13:21), and Mark 9:41 seems to be an exception. In writing about this episode, Mark is touching the heart of the doctrine of Christology—the doctrine of the Person of Jesus Christ. Let us look at a few definitions of the doctrine:

(1) "Christology is the doctrine of the Person of Christ."[1] "The Person of Christ is central in Christian doctrine . . . And the Christological doctrine is central in our theology because Jesus himself is at the centre of all Christian life"[2]

(2) "Christology is that part of Christian doctrine concerned with the revelation of God in Jesus Christ. Traditionally, this has been expressed in the doctrine of the incarnation, the doctrine of the union of the divine and human natures in the one person."[3]

(3) Christology is concerned with the question of the relation between that which is divine and that which is human in the person of Jesus Christ.

Let us turn again to the conversation between Jesus and his disciples. One would say those who saw John the Baptist or Elijah, one of the prophets, in Jesus of Nazareth were only seeing the human nature of Jesus. However, Peter's answer, "You are the Christ," shows he had perceived God's presence in Jesus of Nazareth. He saw more than the human nature of Jesus; he also saw and declared the divine nature of the Christ. In Jesus, the carpenter, the son of Mary, who had brothers and sisters in the town of Nazareth (Mark 6:3), Peter had acknowledged something unique in the person of Jesus—that Jesus was the Christ, the Messiah.

The term *messiah* means the anointed one; in Greek it is *Christos*.[4] In the Hebrew Bible the term *messiah* is applied to the fallowing: (a) The Jewish king (1 Sam. 10:1, 16:13, Ps. 2:2) prior to the Babylonian captivity. (b) After the Babylonian captivity (587 BCE) it referred to a future deliverer of Israel (2 Sam. 7:14–16). Most likely, this was the beginning of the idea of a future *messiah*—a future king such as David. (c) By the time of the New Testament, some Jews expected their future ruler to come as a warrior-king like David; others believed he would come as a supernatural cosmic judge of the earth; and still others, a priestly ruler who would provide authoritative interpretations of God's law for his people.[5]

When Peter answered, "You are the Christ," he meant Jesus was the Lord's anointed one, the Messiah that Israel had been waiting for all that time. However, one of the greatest claims by the Christian community is the belief in Jesus of Nazareth, "Joseph's son" (Luke 4:22), "the son of Mary" (Mark 6:3), who was both divine and human. Hence, generations of Christians have been striving to answer the same question, Who is Jesus Christ? Jesus was interested to hear what the people were saying about him, yet he also wanted to know what his disciples were saying about him. Indeed every believing community has the responsibility to answer the question from the Christ, "But what about you?" Do we see both the human and the divine natures of Jesus Christ as we walk with him daily?

Often, persons who come into contact with Christ or have committed their lives to Christ have a story to share about their experience of

Christ. We find this true in local African Christian churches and among individual disciples. They all have something to say about who Christ is. In this chapter we shall try to answer the question of who Jesus is by looking at both his human nature and divine nature.

The Humanity of Jesus

First, Jesus had a body. "Jesus was born of a woman" (Gal. 4:4–5), and fashioned in the womb of a human mother, and born into helpless infancy (Luke 2:5–7). He had a mother, father, brothers, and sisters (Mark 6:1–6). He was "a descendant of David" or had lineage to David; he was a Jew (Rom. 1:3). In his ministry he would get tired (John 4:6), he slept (Matt. 8:24), got thirsty (John 1928), and was hungry (Matt. 21:18). He died on the cross (Mark 15:37).

Second, Jesus had a soul. Soul is the "spirit of man" or "man's self."[6] He grew in wisdom, stature, and in favour with God (Luke 2:52). He attracted attention from his early ministry (Luke 4:16), and he experienced typical human emotions. For instance, one day when he saw crowds of people who came to see him because of their different needs and problems, he was moved with compassion on them, because they were harassed, and they looked helpless like sheep without a shepherd (Matt. 9:35ff).

Also, one day Jesus visited Mary and Martha, sisters of a deceased brother, Lazarus. When they received him at their home, Jesus is reported to have been deeply moved and troubled in spirit, which led him to weep (John 11:1ff). Jesus of Nazareth, as "the Son" possessed limited knowledge; like anyone else, or even angels in heaven, he had no clue about the end of the age, which the Father alone knew (Mark 13:32). Jesus was also tempted like anyone else. The three Gospel authors share the temptations Jesus faced from the devil in the desert (Matt. 4:1ff, Mark 1:12f, Luke 4:1ff). The author of Hebrews refers to Jesus as the great High Priest "who has been tempted in every way, just as we are . . ." (Heb. 4:15). Jesus suffered the pain of his crucifixion—he cried "with a loud voice . . . and yielded up his spirit" (Matt. 27:50).

Third, Jesus was viewed as a prophet of the kingdom of God (Mark 8:28, Matt. 21:11, 46). Yet, he was different, because he did not have to produce his credentials as did the prophets who told how they received their calling.[7] Many viewed Jesus as a rabbi who proclaimed the divine law and taught it in the synagogues. He gathered disciples, and debated with the scribes in the manner of their profession and under the same authority of scripture.[8]

Fourth, Jesus was born of the Virgin Mary. The idea of virgin birth is foreign in the Old Testament or in Judaism. Some scholars say that the concept was added in the Hellenistic recasting of the story. They suggest that the angel might have "simply informed Joseph that his son was going to be the Messiah."[9] Mark and John could tell the story without the virgin birth, though John has an echo (8:41). Paul who believed in the divinity of Christ, also believed Jesus had come by the normal gateway of birth (Gal. 4:4), and took upon himself manhood with all it entailed of inherited evil (Rom. 8:3, 2 Cor. 5:21, Gal. 3:13, Phil. 2:7). Matthew believed in a virgin birth, as apparently did Luke (Luke 1:34, 3:23). The basis of the doctrine is Isaiah 7:14. (a) In its original Hebrew form the prophecy says, "the young woman." (b) In the Septuagint version it says, "The virgin will be with child and will give birth to a son and will call him Immanuel." Thus the original meaning was changed in the Hellenistic recasting of the prophecy from "a young woman" to "a virgin."

Dibelius makes the point ". . . that the emphasis in the Matthean narrative is not on the virginity of Mary (as in Luke, esp. 1:34) but on the miraculous conception of the child in her womb."[10] "The doctrine has been accepted by many as an expression of truth, rather than literal fact. James Smart, for example, interprets it to mean, in combination with the phrase, 'conceived by the Holy Spirit,' the completeness and unbroken-ness of Jesus' relation with God."[11]

The Divinity of Jesus

The divinity of Jesus is mirrored through his humility. In Jesus the disciples saw what a person is supposed to be, and they also saw the image of God in him. "He is the image of the invisible God" (Matt. 16:16, Col. 1:15).

First, Jesus' divinity was expressed in his activity—his total obedience to God's will enabled him to preach, teach, and heal the sick (Matt. 4:23, Luke 4:18–19).

Second, he was sinless—". . . tempted in every way, just as we are—yet was without sin" (Heb. 4:15). Jesus was sinless because of his divine nature. As much as Jesus was human and was tempted, he was also divine and would not yield to sin.

Third, Jesus wielded authority and power—divine power. (a) He healed the sick and pronounced forgiveness for their sins. For instance, Luke shares the story of a "sinful woman" who had anointed Jesus' feet with perfume in the house of Simon, a Pharisee who had invited Jesus for dinner. Jesus must have known how sinful the woman was by Jewish standards. At the same time, Jesus wanted to recognize what the sinful woman had done to him, and to share the love of God that led to forgiveness and reconciliation. Jesus said to the woman, "Your sins are forgiven . . . Your faith has saved you; go in peace" (Luke 7:48–50). He did so because he was divine—God incarnate. (b) Jesus alone was able to assure his disciples of the gift of the Holy Spirit that his Father had promised through the prophets. So he urged them to stay in Jerusalem for the gift (Luke 24:49, Acts 1:4–5). The disciples received the gift on the day of Pentecost, 28 May 30 CE (Acts 2:4), and on that day the church of Christ was born into existence.

Fourth, Jesus is the Messiah and the Resurrection. Prior to New Testament writings, there is no reference to a future messiah who is to suffer and die for the sins of the people. (a) This was a creation of the Christians as they interpreted the life of the crucified Christ in the light of the scriptures (Ps. 22, 69, Isa. 53). (b) Yet, the term *messiah* does not appear in those passages. Why then, did the early Christians use the resurrection of Jesus as proof that Jesus was the *messiah*? Most likely, it is those who had been convinced that Jesus was the messiah long before his death[12] (Mark 8:29). Jesus refused to be referred to as "the future deliverer of the people of Israel."[13] The concept then was too politically charged.

> But these hopes took on a new life, so to say, when some of Jesus' followers came to believe that he had been raised from the dead. The belief compelled them to re-assert their earlier convictions with even greater vigour; since God had vindicated Jesus, he must be the one they had said he was. The earliest Christian believers were therefore compelled to insist that the messiah, contrary to general expectation, was to die and be raised from the dead, and they began to search their Scriptures for divine proof. Thus began the distinctively Christian notion of the suffering messiah, who died for the sins of the world and was vindicated by God in a glorious resurrection.[14]

Fifth, who is Jesus Christ in the African Church today? Can African Christians trace something of Jesus in the life and acts of God in the past? How about oral tradition stories such as one in the Shona culture: "*Kumandindendinde, Hamadzangu Unganayi*"?

I grew up in a family of three girls and six boys in the Eastern Highlands of Zimbabwe. We were fortunate to grow up in a family that had a grandmother who was a great storyteller. She shared with us all kinds of stories. One story that we often asked her to tell us again and again was the story of one village woman who was accused of practicing witchcraft in the village. Witchcraft is still considered one of the greatest enemies in African communities. The woman was brought before the sub-chief's council for trial. Members of the village who wished to attend such trials were allowed to do so.

The woman's accusers were many, and they all testified against her. Before the chief pronounced the verdict of a serious case such as exercising witchcraft, the accused had to perform a ritual. That ritual was the only means for the accused to prove her innocence. The ritual was for the accused to walk on a long single log placed across a river pool—a pool infested with crocodiles. If she slipped off the log that would confirm her guilt, and that would be the end of her life, as crocodiles would immediately feast on her. If she managed to walk on the log across that pool, that would prove her innocence and no one in the village would accuse her of witchcraft again. As she began her ordeal of crossing that pool—walking on that single log, with all the villagers watching, the poor woman started singing a song:

> *Kumandinde . . . ndinde!*
> *Hama dzangu unganayi,*
> *Kumandinde . . . ndinde!*
> *Muzowona kufa kwangu!*

The words "*Kumandinde . . . ndinde!*" is a cry of a desperate person, making an appeal beyond humanity, probably to the ancestors. "*Hamadzangu unganayi muzoona kufa kwangu*" means that all my relatives come together and witness my death! It is a song packed with deep emotions of sadness, desperation, and hopelessness. But alas, while her accusers watched and hoped that she would slip off the log and into the jaws of waiting and hungry crocodiles, the rest of the villagers joined in singing, with her, her song. That gave her moral support, and at the same time celebrated the occasion as she appealed for justice and mercy from the ancestors and the Creator. She crossed the pool safely, and was vindicated against all her enemies. Thereafter, she was a free woman.

In asking our grandmother about the secret that caused the deliverance of the poor woman from her enemies, the answer came swiftly: "*Midzimu yake*," meaning, it was her ancestors. The significance of the narrative is not necessarily its factuality but its theological insight of the African past—searching for justice, mercy, and tolerance as people lived together. Amidst some social conflict in ancient Africa, the people acknowledged an awareness of the Creator, who is always in absolute control of situations. One could even say African Christians could trace the Christology of the suffering Christ in such African folktales as the one shared above.

The Message in African Christological Titles

"Christology is that part of the Christian doctrine concerned with the revelation of God in Jesus Christ"[15] or "the doctrine of the Person of Christ and the study of it."[16] Christological titles that have arisen in the universal church, including some from the African church, seem to stand begging to be used in conveying what Christ means to the African people. These include: Jesus as brother, kinsman, friend, liberator, *n'anga*, proto-ancestor, and others.

First, Jesus is perceived as a brother in some African Christian circles. Having a brother is an important relationship in the African life experience. In our family, we grew up not wearing shoes. My eldest brother bought me my first pair of shoes when I was in grade six in boarding school. As young boys growing up, we realized the importance of brothers. It was not wise to start a fight if you knew your brother was not there to give you needed support.

This also was true with young girls. If a high school sweetheart started making trouble, she would normally share that not with parents but with a brother. No wonder one would hear women in *Rukwadzano* circles (church women's organization) singing, "*Ndinokumangarira kununa Mukoma Jesus*!" (I will report you to Brother Jesus). Jesus as a brother who is always there to stand with a believer in times of trouble or conflict is a theological insight that identifies who Jesus is by what he does in one's Christian life.

Second, Jesus is perceived as a kinsman. With most Africans, blood relationships begin with the conjugal or nuclear family whose core is the married couple—husband, wife, and their children. Thereafter, there is the extended family that consists of uncles and aunts, cousins, nephews, nieces, and in-laws. Among the Shona, there is a saying, "*Icho wawona idya nehama*," meaning whatever you get, eat with a relative. This saying springs out of the spirit of *ubuntu*—I am because I belong. Again, in times of need often it is one's relatives who give support. Hence, one should not live in isolation from others, even if one considers oneself better off. We all need each other. Consequently, Christians sing hymns and choruses that talk of Jesus as a kinsman.

Third, Jesus is perceived as a friend, a concept African Christians understand well. I had a friendship with a man who passed away in 2015. We had been friends since we were in grade 1, in the 1940s. His oldest sister was married to my uncle, my father's cousin. According to our custom, I was supposed to call my friend "uncle." One day he said to me, "John, I am not your uncle; I am your friend." That friendship was so warm until he passed on. Jesus said to his disciples, "You are my friends . . ." (John 15:14). Many of our African Christians love singing the hymn "What a friend we have in Jesus!" And indeed, Jesus has proved to be a friend in life.

Fourth, Jesus is perceived as liberator. Many Christians in Africa understand the gospel as God's activity of liberating all humanity. Allan Boesak of South Africa is correct in his interpretation when he refers to the Bible, from the Exodus to the resurrection of Jesus, as a record of God's liberating activity.[17] From 1957 to 1994, all African countries were able to attain political independence from their colonial masters. One could see the hand of God in liberating Africa from its oppressors, through Christ. The gospel of Christ brought liberation to the people in many ways: where once twins were sacrificed to death, today twins are embraced as a blessing; where women were not allowed to lead, today we see female pastors, bishops, and presidents. This all has come through Christ the Liberator.

Fifth, Jesus is perceived as the healer (*n'anga*). This aspect of Christ as a healer speaks to the African people directly since it parallels ideas within African religious heritage.[18] Healing is salvation in African Religion. Indeed, a healer is brought into the family because of "unambiguously anti-life forces."[19] These forces in African society are not perceived as separate, because they mutually interact.[20] For the sake of clarity, Magesa, a well-known Catholic theologian in East Africa understands these anti-life forces as "wrongdoing (wrong actions), illness, and witchcraft."[21] Jesus brings to the individual and community total healing—removing from the mind one's desires to continue with wrongdoing, from the body the pain of illness, and from the spirit the fear of witchcraft. That is the kind of salvation Africans have been looking for all along. Many people are hurting and need healing for the whole person. Jesus is the healer who brings both newness (2 Cor. 5:17) and wholeness (John 10:10) to lives.

Sixth, Jesus is perceived as a proto-ancestor. The word *proto* is often combined with another, and means "first in time" or "first in importance."[22] One would never understand African Religion without understanding the concept and role of ancestors in African thought and life. The major role of an ancestor is mediating between the living and community of the "living-dead," or those in the after-death community. In the Shona culture and African Religion, when a man offers prayers to the Creator, he does so through the ancestors. He will address prayer first through his father—call upon him by his name, then his grandfather's name, and his great-grandfather's name. If he cannot remember some of the names, he will ask those ancestors he can name to pass on his petitions and requests to other ancestors who came before them so that his prayer reaches the Creator. In this hierarchical arrangement, one always wants to think that there is the proto-ancestor. Although one does not know his name, he is important because he is the one nearer to the Creator who can deliver the family's and community's petitions. Now, African theology is identifying that unknown proto-ancestor as Jesus Christ. He is our Mediator with God the Father.

Today, some African preachers have craftily used some of the Christological titles mentioned above and others in their communication of the gospel of Jesus Christ. Jesus asks, "But who do you say I am?" The African Christian communities respond resoundingly: You are our brother, our kinsman, our friend, our liberator, our healer (*n'anga*), and our proto-ancestor.

Chapter 7

The Holy Spirit

The Holy Spirit is a favourite doctrine of many Christians in Africa and a favourite doctrine as a subject for preaching by many African preachers. It is also a most misunderstood and abused doctrine by many Christian believers. Thank God that in spite of our shortcomings in understanding the doctrine of the Holy Spirit fully, every Sunday as we meet for worship, we affirm our faith as Christians, according to the Nicene Creed, saying, "We believe in the Holy Spirit, the Lord, the giver of life, who proceeds from the Father and the Son, who with the Father and the Son, is worshipped and glorified, who has spoken through the prophets."[1]

Some think that the Holy Spirit is absent from the Old Testament. That is not correct. Instead, we can say that the role of the Holy Spirit in the Old Testament seems different from that in the New Testament.

The Spirit of God in the Old Testament

The Bible teaches that all creation was made through the Word (Christ) (John 1:3); and that at the beginning of creation, while "the earth was formless and empty, darkness was over the surface of the deep (Gen. 1:1–2). Meanwhile, the Spirit of God hovered over the waters, giving life and meaning to creation. So we can see that the Holy Spirit is co-eternal with the Father and the Son; he has always existed. We begin to learn more about him in the Old Testament testimonies, where he was known primarily as the Spirit of God (Gen. 1:2), who manifested himself in a number of ways. He seemed to be the power and illumination that God gave as he wished.[2]

In Hebrew, spirit is *ruach*, which means wind (Exod. 10:13), breath (Gen. 6:17), or divine power (Ezek. 37:9f).[3] In the Old Testament the word *spirit* is rarely prefaced by the adjective "holy," except in Isaiah 63:10, 11 and Psalms 51:11.[4] Rather, he is often identified as the Spirit of God or the Spirit of the Lord.

One thing I have noticed about preaching in African churches is that when the preacher preaches on a man or woman of the Spirit of God, he/she often chooses an Old Testament character. This shows that the Old Testament has a lot to teach us about the Spirit of God.

William Barclay makes the following points about the Holy Spirit in the Old Testament: First, the Spirit is the agent of God in creation. In Genesis, we have already noted how the Spirit of God was hovering over the waters (Gen. 1:2). Further, listen to Elihu's affirmation of creation by the Spirit. Elihu was one of the three friends worried and concerned about Job's situation. Because he was younger than Job, he did not want to say anything as the other two friends had, but eventually he did speak: "I am young in years, and you are old . . ." (Job 32:6). And again, "The Spirit of the Lord has made me; the breath of the Almighty gives me life" (Job 33:4).

Second, the great leaders of the Old Testament are people who possess the Spirit or who have been possessed by the Spirit, and in whom the Spirit dwells. Recall how Joseph effectively interpreted the dreams of Pharaoh concerning a famine that was to come. In his interpretation of the dream, Joseph pointed out that disaster could be avoided if careful planning was carried out. As if turning to his council, Pharaoh asked rhetorically, "Can we find anyone like this man, one in whom is the spirit of God?" (Gen. 41:38).

Third, in the Old Testament the Spirit of God is specially connected with the gift and the obligation of prophecy. For example, with Saul, "the Spirit of God came powerfully upon him, and he joined in their prophesying" (1 Sam. 10:10). We also have a personal testimony of the prophet Ezekiel who says, "Then the Spirit of the Lord came on me, and he told me to say . . ." (Ezek. 11:5).

Fourth, the fact remains that in general the work of the Spirit is connected with the extraordinary and the abnormal. The tremendous feats of strength of Samson are attributed to the Spirit of the Lord (Judg. 13:25, 14:6, 19, 15:14). The experience of the Spirit is not for the common person or for every day.[5]

Fifth, the Spirit is treated as the promise of God for future generations of God's people in Old Testament prophecy. The prophet Ezekiel delivered such a profound message of a new covenant of God with Israel when he said, "I will give you a new heart and put a new spirit in you; I will remove from you your heart of stone and give you a heart of flesh. And I will put my Spirit in you . . ." (Ezek. 36:26–27). Joel's prophecy stands out prominently: "I will pour out my Spirit on all people. Your sons and daughters will prophesy, your old men will dream dreams, your young men will see visions" (Joel 2:28).

The Holy Spirit Poured Out on All People

First, let's look at the Holy Spirit in the Gospels. (a) In reading the four Gospels, one finds that the Spirit of God was active in Jesus' life—his birth, his baptism, his overcoming temptations in the desert, his whole ministry as he moved back and forth between Galilee and Judea teaching, preaching, healing, exorcising demons, challenging the Jewish leaders to serve the poor, the sick, and the oppressed. The Spirit also is active in the transfiguration story, in Jesus' unwavering determination to die on the cross, his resurrection, and the ascension. It was all life in the Spirit.

(b) Jesus taught his disciples about the Holy Spirit in the Gospels, especially in the Gospel of John, in chapters 14, 15, and 16. In those passages, Jesus says the Holy Spirit would be their *Parakletos* or Paraclete, translated Counsellor, Comforter, Advocator, or Helper (14:16,

14:26, 15:26, 16:7). According to the Gospel of John, Jesus in his teaching emphasized that: (i) the Holy Spirit is the gift of God in Jesus Christ (John 14:16); (ii) the Holy Spirit is the abiding presence of the Risen Lord (John 16:7); (iii) the Spirit comes to him who loves God, and who keeps God's commands: "If you love me, keep my commands . . ." (John 14:15); (iv) the Spirit is the teacher of truth—One who teaches all things (John 14:26); and (v) the Holy Spirit has a witnessing, convincing, and a convicting work (John 15:26, 16:8–11).[6]

More importantly, before ascending to the Father, Jesus appeared to his disciples over a period of forty days, and taught them about the kingdom of God. On one occasion Jesus gave them this command: "Do not leave Jerusalem, but wait for the gift my Father promised, which you have heard me speak about. For John baptized with water, but in a few days you will be baptized with the Holy Spirit" (Acts 1:4–5).

He also assured his disciples that they would receive power when the Holy Spirit had come; and that they would be his witnesses beginning in "Jerusalem, and in all Judea and Samaria, and to the ends of the earth" (Acts 1:8). As he was talking to them, suddenly Jesus was "taken up before their very eyes" (Acts 1:9) into heaven, at the hill called the Mount of Olives. Apparently, this group of about one hundred and twenty disciples, who "joined together constantly in prayer" (Acts 1:14), included the apostles, the women, Mary the mother of Jesus, and Jesus' brothers (Acts 1:12–14). All were witnesses of the ascension event. Note that the brothers of Jesus, who had seemed to be among his opponents (Mark 3:21), or whom John says did not believe in Jesus (John 8:5), witnessed Jesus' glorious departure just after he had confirmed that they would all become his witnesses to the ends of the earth (Acts 1:8–9). Immediately afterward, they all left for Jerusalem. When they arrived back in Jerusalem, they went upstairs to the room in which they were staying. Mathias was elected to take the place of Judas Iscariot.

Second, we'll examine the day of Pentecost. William Barclay points out that there were three Jewish festivals that every male living within twenty miles of Jerusalem was expected to attend—Passover, Pentecost, and the Feast of Tabernacles. The Feast of Passover commemorated the exodus of the children of Israel from their slavery in Egypt (Exod. 13:10), and was celebrated in the middle of April.[7] The Feast of Tabernacles was the Israelite Harvest Thanksgiving Festival, which was also known as the Feast of Booths. It commemorated God's protection of the people during their wanderings in the wilderness (Lev. 23:39–43) as they travelled to the Promised Land. This Feast was celebrated 15–22 September.[8]

The term *Pentecost* means The Fiftieth. Another name for Pentecost Feast was The Feast of Weeks. It was so-called because Pentecost fell on the fiftieth day, a week of weeks, after the Passover, at the beginning of June.[9] While there were other small festivals that the Jews observed, these three festivals drew great crowds of Jews to Jerusalem from all over the known nations of the time. People who came to Jerusalem from far away countries for one festival could easily stay for the other festival before returning home. For the Pentecost of 28 May 30 CE, the disciples had had the Last Supper with Jesus in the upper room, a place they continued to meet, waiting for what Jesus through the Father had promised—the gift of the Holy Spirit.

(a) The occasion was the day of Pentecost. As Luke points out, when the day of Pentecost had come, the disciples "were all together in one place." Most likely that place was the upper room. That particular upper room could have been in the house of the mother of John Mark. It is also suggested that in that same house Jesus and his disciples had celebrated his Last Supper. Later on, after Peter had been rescued from prison by an angel, he went to the house of Mary, the mother of John Mark (Acts 12:12), which had become the headquarters of the Christian church in Jerusalem.[10] If that was the house in which they waited for the gift of the Holy Spirit, it means after receiving the Holy Spirit they came down in the streets, speaking with tongues. Another possibility is that they could have been situated within the temple precincts.[11]

(b) "Suddenly a sound like the blowing of a violent wind came from heaven and filled the whole house where they were sitting" (Acts 2:2). Frederick Bruner points out how essential it is to understand the usage of several key words in the above sentence by Luke—*suddenly* and *from heaven*. It appears the disciples had just congregated in the room on the day of Pentecost, when "suddenly" the gift—the Holy Spirit—appeared from heaven,[12] giving "the Holy Spirit his proper direction of origin and tak[ing] the source of the gift from men's hands and hearts."[13] There is no mention that the disciples were kneeling or praying or singing. Instead, the coming of the Holy Spirit on the day of Pentecost was God's doing, God's gift to those who believed in his Son, Jesus Christ. Lest human beings boast that they had prayed for the Holy Spirit to come, the Holy Spirit, God's promised gift to the followers of Christ, came suddenly and from heaven.[14]

"They saw what seemed to be tongues of fire that separated and came to rest on each of them" (Acts 2:3). C. S. C. Williams says, "As the divine presence or *Shekinah* rested on the pious Jew studying the Law, and as Paul hoped that the power of Christ would rest on him (2 Cor. 12:9), so the purifying and consuming flame of the Holy Spirit rested on each apostle."[15] The Holy Spirit manifested himself in the "sudden wind" that filled the whole house, and in the fire that rested on every person in the room.

(c) "All were filled with the Holy Spirit and began to speak in other tongues as the Spirit enabled them" (Acts 2:4). According to Williams, the word *all* probably refers to the Twelve.[16] Richard Rackham says the violent wind "sounded through the whole house, for the hundred and twenty [and suggesting they] must have occupied more than one chamber."[17] He maintains the followers of Christ that had probably witnessed the ascension of Jesus into heaven (Acts 1:15) were in the room.

"All of them were filled with the Holy Spirit . . ." (2:4a), or they were baptized by the Holy Spirit. Everyone in that room experienced a new awareness of the presence of God, the Holy Spirit, and acknowledged that they had been filled with the Holy Spirit. Those in the room must have realized and accepted that the promised gift of the Father, through the Christ exalted to the right hand of God, had finally been poured upon them as Joel had prophesied (Joel 2:28). The Holy Spirit was given on that day, not partially or conditionally, but in full.[18] He was given once and for all times, including to future generations. Thus, the Holy Spirit must be received in full, and everyone is worthy of the gift. A person who is confronted by Jesus Christ is always left on the path to transformation and development in the new life of love and service to others—loving God and loving neighbour through the power of the Spirit.

It is always important to remember that the "power of the baptism of the Holy Spirit is the power of *Christocentricity*."[19] Those of the Wesleyan heritage call this Christian phenomenon in a believer "growing toward perfection."

Following the outpouring of the Holy Spirit, Luke wrote: ". . . [they] began to speak in other tongues as the Spirit enabled them" (Acts 2:4). There were in Jerusalem God-fearing or devout Jews who had come from every nation under heaven for the celebration of the Festival of Pentecost. Luke puts those God-fearing Jews into three categories: (i) Jews who lived to the east of Judea and spoke Aramaic, including Parthians, Medes, and Elamites; (ii) residents of Mesopotamia, Cappadocia, Pontus and Asia Minor, Phrygia and Pamphylia, Egypt and parts of Libya near Cyrene; and (iii) visitors from Rome, both Jews and proselytes, who were the only contingent from the European mainland, and Cretans and Arabs. F. F. Bruce points out that even if Greece is not mentioned, it must have been represented.[20] Similarly, John Chrysostom of Antioch also says that although Ethiopia is not mentioned, it was represented.

Most of the Jews who came to Jerusalem probably understood Aramaic, the language of their homeland, but it is possible that some did not. It must have been particularly the Jewish pilgrims, who after hearing "this sound" came together in bewilderment (Acts 2:6). There are two possible interpretations concerning "this sound." They could have heard the sound of the rushing wind, and the ensuing sound of glorifying God. F. F. Bruce writes, "Many of them were astonished as they heard the loud praises of God uttered by the disciples in inspired language—for this, rather than the rushing noise wind, is what is meant by 'this sound' in v. 6—because they recognized the indigenous languages and dialects of their native lands."[21] They heard the apostles declaring the wonders of God in their own tongues or languages. "Utterly amazed, they asked: 'Aren't all these who are speaking Galileans? Then how is it that each of us hears them in our native language?" (Acts 2:7–8).

It may be helpful to take heed of Bruner when he wrote:

> It appears to be Luke's opinion, expressed at least in his choice of words, that the event at Pentecost was unique in being a "speaking in other (*heterais*) tongues," i.e. in other languages (cf. the synonym in vv. 6 and 8: *dialekto*). In neither of the other two (and only) records of *glossolalia* in Acts does Luke add the word "other" to tongues (cf. 10:46, 19:6). Furthermore, there was no one recorded as present at either Caesarea (Acts 10) or Ephesus (Acts 19) who needed a speaking in other tongues; only at Pentecost do we have a record, as Luke intends it, of several diverse linguistic groups to whom the gospel is preached by means of miraculously given tongues.[22]

Bruce also shares that:

> When the law was given at Sinai, according to the rabbinic tradition, the ten commandments were promulgated with a single sound, yet it says all the people perceived the voices (Exod. 20:18);[23] this shows that when the voice went forth it was divided into seven voices and then went

> into seventy tongues, and every people received the law in their own language.[24]

Thus, on the anniversary of the lawgiving, Pentecost, again people from every nation were enabled to hear the gospel of Jesus Christ proclaimed in their own language without an interpreter.

(d) In addressing the crowd, Peter made it clear that Jesus of Nazareth was a man accredited by God to them by his miracles; yet with the help of the wicked, Jews decided to nail him on the cross. Peter went on to point out that God raised Jesus to life—exalted him to the right hand of God. Seated at the right hand of God, the Father had made him both Lord and Christ. That same Christ received from the Father the promise, the gift of the Holy Spirit who had been poured out for this audience to see and hear. Hearing that challenging message, the people asked, "What shall we do?"

Peter replied that repentance and baptism in the name of Christ were needed to receive forgiveness of sin, and the gift of the Holy Spirit. Those who accepted the message repented and were baptized, and up to three thousand were added to the number of disciples of Jesus Christ. On that day the church of Christ was born into existence. That newly born church of Christ had been endowed with the gift of the Holy Spirit, a gift given once and for all.

Peter assured his listeners that day that the promise or the gift of the Holy Spirit from the Father through Christ was given for all those that had been baptized in the name of Christ on that day and their children and for all who were far off—for all whom the Lord our God would call (Acts 2:22–39).

The Holy Spirit in the Expanding Church

According to John, during his ministry Jesus prioritized doing the will of his Father and finishing the work for which he was sent (John 4:34, 5:36). And before giving up his spirit on the cross, he uttered his last words,

"It is finished" (John 19:30). Jesus died a victor for he had accomplished what he came to do. He had assured his disciples, "I will not leave you as orphans; I will come to you" (John 14:18). Jesus' words related to the coming of the Spirit; he also spoke of his appearances after the resurrection and at his second coming (see John 14:3, 19, 28, 16:22).[25] Jesus went on to say, "But when he, the Spirit of truth, comes . . . He will not speak on his own; he will speak only what he hears . . ." (John 16:13). We are not told whether he hears from the Father or the Son, for the verse stresses the close relationship among the three[26]—the Father, the Son, and the Holy Spirit. Such sayings by John on Jesus' teaching about the Holy Spirit enable us to understand the relationship of Jesus and the Holy Spirit, as well as the Holy Spirit and the church.

Now, let us turn to the matter of relationships. First, the Holy Spirit was a gift from the Father through Jesus Christ to the church. This gift of the Holy Spirit should not be confused with the gifts of the Spirit. Bruce clearly makes the distinction: "The gift of the Spirit is the Spirit Himself, bestowed by the Father through the Messiah; the gifts of the Spirit are those spiritual faculties which the Spirit imparts, 'dividing to each one severally even as he will'" (1 Cor. 12:11).[27]

In speaking about the "Day of the Lord" Joel had proclaimed God's message saying, "And afterward, I will pour out my Spirit on all people" (Joel 2:28). Jesus clearly articulated this message on one occasion as he ate with his disciples, saying, "Do not leave Jerusalem, but wait for the gift my Father promised, which you have heard me speak about" (Acts 1:4). Earlier on in this chapter, we noted that in the Old Testament era, the Spirit of God was apportioned to certain categories of people. But then after Jesus' death on the cross, his resurrection, and ascension to his Father, where he is exalted to the right hand of God, he received from the Father the promised Holy Spirit, which he poured out on Peter's audience on that day of Pentecost (Acts 2:33). What a gift to the church!

The Holy Spirit came especially for the "origin and development of the church in the world."[28] Jesus Christ had already laid the foundation for his church through his life, ministry, his death on the cross, and his resurrection from the dead. As Paul rightly observed, "For no one can lay any foundation other than the one already laid, which is Jesus Christ" (1 Cor. 3:11). Thus, the Holy Spirit was to act as a midwife—enabling the birth of the church of Christ into the world on the day of Pentecost in Jerusalem on 28 May 30 CE.

Second, the Father through Jesus Christ gave the Holy Spirit, the Spirit of truth, to the individual followers of Christ. According to John, Jesus had instructed his disciples:

> "If you love me, keep my commands. And I will ask the Father, and he will give you another advocate to help you and be with you forever—the Spirit of truth. The world cannot accept him, because it neither sees him nor knows him. But you know him, for he lives with you and will be in you." (John 14:15–17)

What is significant in this text is the difference between "with you" and "in you." Merrill Tenney points this out:

> The difference between *with you* and *in you* (17) is significant, for it shows that whereas the Spirit was watching over the disciples at the time when Jesus spoke, a crisis was coming when the Spirit would enter into the lives of the disciples and control them from within.[29]

That means from the day of Pentecost the gift of the Holy Spirit was not only given to the church of Christ, but also to every disciple who repented of his/her sins and was baptized in the name of Christ. Each would receive both forgiveness of sins and the gift of the Holy Spirit as the indwelling Spirit. Hence, Paul is saying to the Christian community in Rome, "You, however, are not in the realm of the flesh but are in the realm of the Spirit, if indeed the Spirit of God lives in you" (Rom. 8:9).

Third, the Holy Spirit divinely empowered the newly born church corporately and the believers individually. Jesus had promised the disciples they would receive power when the Holy Spirit comes upon them (Acts 1:8). Thus, the disciples were both filled and empowered by the Holy Spirit. One would only need to turn to Peter's sermon on the day of Pentecost to understand and appreciate the change that came to the disciples on that day. With the support of the eleven disciples standing with him, Peter boldly proclaimed in the Temple this message: Jesus of Nazareth was handed over to Israel "by God's set purpose and foreknowledge. Israel instigated the Romans to put him to death by nailing him on the cross. God then raised that Jesus to life, and they were witnesses to that fact. Jesus subsequently ascended into heaven, and God exalted him to his right hand, making him both Lord and Christ—the Messiah. That empowered message enabled three thousand converts to be baptized and added to the church of Christ on that day.

Fourth, the promise of the gift of the Holy Spirit—and especially, the inward presence or the indwelling Spirit—was "for all whom the Lord our God will call" (Acts 2:39). Peter's message on the Day of Pentecost was that the gift of the Holy Spirit was not only limited to those in attendance at Pentecost in Jerusalem. Rather, it was to their descendants also. And not just the Jews, but also the Gentiles who were far off, and to all future generations of believers in all lands, whom the Lord will call. Because the church of Christ would be empowered by the Holy Spirit, it would reach every continent of the earth. Bruce notices that in this message of Peter two Old Testament passages are brought together: (a) "'Peace, peace, to those far and near,' says the Lord. 'And I will heal them'" (Isa. 57:19), and (b) "And everyone who calls on the name of the Lord will be saved" (Joel 2:32).[30]

Chapter 8

The Holy Trinity

The term *trinity* refers to the "Christian doctrine of the triune God. The Trinity is not explicitly mentioned in the NT: it was defined as a result of continuous exploration of the biblical data."[1] Or the term *trinity* represents the crystallization of the New Testament teaching concerning the co-existence of the Godhead—the Father, the Son, and the Holy Spirit.[2] It is essential to understand the circumstances under which the doctrine of the Trinity came into existence. It was the first controversy within the Christian faith in the fourth century. Its main concern was with the question of the unity of God in the context of the Christian faith.

Biblical Foundation of the Doctrine of the Trinity

First, the Old Testament scriptures are clear concerning the teaching on the oneness of God. The first commandment states: "I am the Lord your God, who brought you out of Egypt, out of the land of slavery. You shall have no other gods before me" (Exod. 20:2–3). And from Deuteronomy, "Hear, O Israel: the Lord our God, the Lord is one. Love the Lord your God with all your heart and with all your soul and with all your strength (Deut. 6:4–5).

Second, the early Christians also believed in the oneness of the Lord their God. In answering one of the teachers of the law who had asked Jesus about the most important law, Jesus quoted the Deuteronomic text, and added to it: "The most important one . . . is this: 'Hear, O Israel, the Lord our God, the Lord is one. Love the Lord your God with all your heart and with all your soul and with all your mind and with all your strength.' The second is this: 'Love your neighbor as yourself.' There is no commandment greater than these" (Mark 12:29–31).

We can see that Jesus is quoting from two scripture sources: (a) The first quotation is from Deuteronomy 6:4–5, which came to be known as the *Shema*; and the term *Shema* came from the first word of Deuteronomy 6:4 in Hebrew, which means "hear." The *Shema* became the Jewish confession of faith that was recited by pious Jews every morning and evening. To this day it begins every synagogue sermon.[3] (b) The second quotation of Jesus' answer comes from Leviticus 19:18, which says: "Do not seek revenge or bear a grudge against anyone among your people, but love your neighbor as yourself. I am the Lord."[4]

Third, despite Christians' understanding of the oneness of the Lord their God in the Jewish faith, a new situation arose as J. L. Nerve says: "It began with the overwhelming conviction confirmed by Scripture, that the presence of Christ in the Church is like that of God the Father himself. The early Christians prayed to Christ as they prayed to God."[5]

We do see Christian scriptures from which the whole idea of the triune God emerged. For example, Paul, who was converted to Christianity about 33–34 CE, and made three notable missionary journeys to a number of provinces within the Roman Empire, visiting some of the leading cities of the time between 46 and 58 CE,[6] had the habit of revisiting and writing the churches he had founded. In some of his letters to such churches, the first Christian literature to circulate among the Christian communities, Paul used several correlations of the three persons of the Trinity. For instance, "There are different kinds of gifts, but the same Spirit . . . the same Lord . . . the same God (1 Cor. 12:4–6), and "There is . . . one Spirit . . . one Lord . . . one God (Eph. 4:4–6). In his benediction he wrote, "May the grace of the Lord Jesus Christ, and the love of God, and the fellowship of the Holy Spirit be with you all" (2 Cor. 13:14).

Similarly, with the baptismal rite, which on the day of Pentecost was pronounced in the name of Jesus Christ (Acts 2:38), by the time

Matthew wrote his Gospel (in the late 50s CE, or the 60s, or 70s) the Great Commission commands baptism in the name of God, "the Father and of the Son and of the Holy Spirit" (Matt. 28:19).

Thus the question that confronted Christianity in the third century was, Had Christians abandoned the idea of monotheism (one God) to that of tritheism (three gods)? That became the Trinitarian controversy that the church had to resolve.

Meaning of the Doctrine of the Trinity

First, what is the message of the doctrine of the Trinity? What does it really mean? What the doctrine of the Trinity says to Christians is that on the stage of human experience God has revealed himself to humanity in history in three roles. Harold DeWolf said that (a) Christians testify that they have known God as the eternal Father, the Creator and Judge in whom all the order and the very being of the world, the moral law, and all truth are grounded[7]; (b) Christians would also claim that they know God as the Son, the God who humbled himself in love for his children, speaking at definite times in history, through specific human beings and supremely through Jesus Christ his transforming Word[8]; and (c) further, Christians would claim knowing God as the Holy Spirit, the sacred presence within themselves, binding them to God and to their fellow believers with cords of love, opening their eyes to the evidence of God as Creator and Judge, reminding them of his revealing pasts in history, summoning them to faith through Jesus Christ and empowering them to obey the divine commands they have heard.[9] This is what the doctrine of the Trinity means, and what it is saying.

Second, the dictionary meaning of the term *trinity* (Latin, *trinitas*, *triad*) is the condition of being three or threefold or a set of three persons or things that form a unit. The term *trinitas* was coined by Tertullian (160–220 CE), a great African theologian and author who also provided the fundamental formula for the trinity and Christology when he said, "Let us preserve the mystery of divine economy, which disposes [to place in a certain order] the unity into trinity, the Father, the Son, and the Holy Spirit, three not in essence [power of being] but in grade, not in substance but in form."[10]

Third, understanding the word *economy* in ancient Christian theology is important for it means "God 'building up' his manifestation in periods of history."[11] That means in the Trinity there is one divine essence (power of being), and each of the three economic manifestations of the power of being participates in the full power of being.[12]

Fourth, the meaning of the "person": (a) The One God is known as Father, Son, and Holy Spirit; each is God but a distinct person. Thus, we are talking of "the coexistence of Father, Son, and the Holy Spirit in the unity of the Godhead."[13] (b) Note that each one of the three economic manifestations of the One God are referred to as persons—"God in three persons, Blessed Trinity," we sing. (c) "In our personality there is one centre, the self; but in God there are three personal centres in eternal and perfect harmony (John 15:26f, 17:21) . . ." (d) All three make up the being of him who is in himself Maker, Savior, and Inspirer. They were careful to add that the three 'roles' were not passing appearances but eternal facts of God."[14]

Fifth, the purpose of the doctrine: (a) "The doctrine of the Trinity rightly affirms that God the Father is the ground of all existence, all truth and hope, that Jesus Christ, the Son of God is his Word Incarnate, and that the Holy Spirit is our present Comforter, guide and enabling power."[15] (b) "The purpose of the ancient church's doctrine of the Trinity is to maintain both the definitive and dynamic content and the unity of the Christian faith in God."[16] That faith is the "greatest commandment" (Mark 12:29).

Process of Formation of the Doctrine of the Trinity

First, we will discuss the early stages in the development of the Trinitarian conception of God. As the early Christians prayed to Christ and to God, church leaders were motivated to understand the relation of

Christ to the belief in One God. On the other hand, we have already pointed out that there also existed the Trinitarian baptismal formula in the Gospel of Matthew and in the letters of Paul. Originally, some leaders felt that Christ was the Son of God and ascribed to him those attributes of a son. Baur and Harnack say that the early Christians, particularly Hermas, held the Ebionitic or adoptionistic views. Ebonitism was part of what came to be known as a heretical Judaizing Christianity. First, it emphasized Jewish nationality and the Law; and second, it rejected the virgin birth and taught that Jesus was merely a man, on whom the Holy Spirit had descended for the first time at his baptism by John the Baptist. That was the reason such Christians were understood as Ebionitic or Adoptinistic.[17] Their language was frequently binitarian (binitarianism is the belief that there are only two persons in the godhead, in contrast to three, the orthodox doctrine).[18] The Spirit was taken as the Spirit of Christ (2 Cor. 3:17). The early apologists, in their aim at creating a Christian theology, discussed more or less the relationship between Father and Son. They introduced the Logos term from St. John's Gospel. Irenaeus in his conflict with Gnosticism taught without speculation and simply on the basis of the Rule of Faith that Son and Spirit participate in the Divine substance.

Second, it was Tertullian who first defined God as the Father, Son, and Holy Spirit: (a) To express his thought he used the word *trinitas*. (b) He championed *hypostasianism* (the idea that God revealed himself in three persons) against the *mornarchiasm* (the idea that there is only One God).[19] (c) Tertullian used analogies that showed *surbodinationism*; for example, "The Father, Son, and Holy Spirit are each other as the root, shrub, and tree; and same fountain, stream, and river."[20] Or, "the word proceeds from God, just as the beam proceeds from the sun."[21] Tillich goes on to say, "The idea of three *hypostaseis*, three different personae, could lead to *tritheism*."[22] (d) The problem, presented in two questions: (i) "How could the Church escape from surbodinationism? Or how could it get away from the view of Christ as a kind of a "second God"?

(ii) How could the Trinity of special persons (*hypostassianism*) be maintained without sacrificing Christian monotheism?[23]

Third, the Arian Controversy: At the beginning of the fourth century, the debate concerning the relation of God the Father and the Son heated up in the church. The more Christians worshiped Jesus Christ as God, the more they wanted clarification whether Christianity then still worshiped one God or two. Further, they wanted to know the relation between God the Father and God the Son.

Arius was a presbyter or elder in the Christian community of Alexandria, Egypt (256–336 CE). He was a man held in high esteem for his zeal and integrity[24]; and in 319 CE, he aroused interest in the church by teaching that: (a) only God the Father is eternal and unoriginated[25]; (b) "The Son [Logos] was created, and not made—there was once when he was not; the very fact that he was Son proved that he could not be equal with the Father."[26] (c) Christ was demigod or *demiurge*—"half God and half man."[27] According to the *Collins Concise English Dictionary*, "demigod is a minor deity; or the offspring of a human being and a god or goddess; a godlike person.[28] Concerning a demiurge, in Greek *demiourgos means skilled workman or craftsman, or creator.* In *Plato's philosophy deity is the creator of the universe; in Gnostic philosophy, the creator of the universe is subordinate to the supreme deity.* Both *demigod and demiurge are* half God and half man. Thus Arius was saying, Christ is half God and half man.

(d) According to Arius' teaching, the Logos or Word of God or Son of God entered "a body without a soul" and by so doing, Arius had challenged the "the belief in Christ's true humanity."[29]

Athanasius was a young man, a deacon in the Christian community of Alexandria (298–373 CE), who opposed Arius' views on the relation of Christ to God the Father. His views were: (a) If Christ is divine, then "he belongs to the unseparated, undivided monad [unit] of the Deity." (b) Thus the co-eternity and the co-equality of the Son with the Father must follow. (c) If Christ is a demigod, such as a *demiurge* of the Gnostics, then we are worshipping a creature. (d) "There could only be a full redemption if the Redeemer be one fully divine."[30] (e) "Upon these thoughts only could he base prayer to Christ, the administration of baptism, and above all, the redemptive character of the Christian religion with the forgiveness of sin and the hope of the resurrection."[31]

Fourth, the Council of Nicaea 325: The Council was opened by an appeal from the Emperor for peace. (a) After much debate, Eusebius of Caesarea brought forward the traditional Baptismal Confession of his church. It declared faith "in the one Lord, Jesus Christ, the Word of God, God from God, Light from Light, Life from Life, Only-begotten Son, first born of all creation, before the ages begotten from the father." (b) For quite some time, the debate had been on the words *homoousion* (of same essence or substance) and *homoiousion* (of like substance),[32] or similar; which would have meant, "the Father and Son are equal in every respect, but they do not have the identical substance."[33] These two Greek words are from the word *ousia*, which means one essence.[34] After some debate, the Emperor, most likely by advice from Hosius, the Bishop of Cordova, personally proposed the word "*homoousion*," meaning "of the same essence."

Decision of the Council of Nicaea 325: (a) Arius's Christology was rejected and condemned. (b) The main decision that was adopted was that Christ is "of the same substance with the Father."[35] Thus, the Nicene Creed begins:

> We believe in one God, the Father Almighty, Maker of all things visible and invisible . . . And in one Lord Jesus Christ, the Son of God, begotten of the Father, the only-begotten of the essence of the Father, God of God, and Light of Light, true God of true God, begotten not made, being of one substance [*homoousios*] with the Father, by whom all things were made in heaven and on earth, who for us men and our salvation came down and was incarnate and was made man. He suffered and on the third day he rose again,

> ascended into heaven. From thence he comes to judge the quick and the dead. And in the Holy Ghost.[36]

(c) A statement of condemnation: "And those who say there was a time when he was not, or he was not before he was made, and he was made out of nothing, and out of another substance or thing, or the Son of God is created or changeable, or alterable, they are condemned by the Catholic Church."[37] While the central phrase is "of the same substance with the Father," nothing of the sort is said of the Holy Spirit.[38]

Significance of the decision of the Nicaea Council 325: According to Paul Tillich, "The most serious Christian heresy was overcome. Christ is not one of the many half-gods; he is not a hero. He is God himself appearing in divine essence within a historical person." (b) The confession of Nicaea was expressed in terms more pleasing to Rome and the West than to the East. The East did not like the *homoousios*; instead it wanted a ladder of hierarchies. (c) The decisive statement is: "Being of one substance with the Father." (d) "Jesus Christ is not an incarnated half-god; he is not a creature above all others; he is God. And God is creator and unconditioned."[39]

Fifth, at the Council of Constantinople, 381, the following decision concerning the Trinity was reached: (a) The Council of Constantinople removed the condemnations that had been added to the Creed of Nicaea. (b) The Council also said something about the Holy Spirit, who was not included at Nicaea. Thus the following statement was added: "And in the Holy Spirit, the Lord and Giver of Life, who proceedeth from the Father, who with the Father and the Son together is worshipped and glorified."[40] This decision ends the Trinitarian struggle.

Chapter 9

The Atonement

The word *atonement* comes from the verb to atone, meaning to make amends for wrongdoing[1]; and *atonement* means "satisfaction given for wrong doing."[2] There are several definitions of atonement in Christian theology, and they all seem to agree. We shall look at a few definitions:

(1) "Atonement in Christian theology means the amending of the broken relationships between God and man caused by sin, and the release of man from his bondage to freedom through the grace of God."[3]

(2) "Generally, the term refers to the reconciliation (at-one-ment) of two parties. In Christian theology, it refers to the restoration of the broken relation between God and man that was accomplished in the life and death of Jesus Christ."[4]

(3) "Sin destroys the relationship between God and people, and atonement is the means by which reconciliation is effected."[5]

The Need for Atonement

From time immemorial, humanity has always experienced the need for atonement. We live in a broken world full of broken nations, families, and even personalities. It appears the forces of conflict and tensions among nations are increasing with each passing day. Nations and international organizations are thrown into chaos, at times by leaders who want to remain in office by using their own powers instead of by the power of the ballot box. Countries are failing to reach their economic potential or attain peace because of policies that benefit only a few people. Corruption seems rampant left and right in many nations and organizations, including Christian organizations like the church. We fail to live up to others' expectations.

Saint Paul was correct when he wrote to the Roman Christian community: "'There is no one righteous, not even one; there is no one who understands; there is no one who seeks God. All have turned away, they have together become worthless; there is no one who does good, not even one . . . There is no fear of God before their eyes'" (Rom. 3:10–18).

The problem and need for atonement is a worldwide challenge to all humanity—individuals, families, extended families, communities, nations, and as international regions.

First, in the Shona culture of Zimbabwe, there is a psycho-religious traditional practice that is performed to this day. It happens with persons who out of anger or other motivations assault a parent. Take for instance a young man who beats his mother because the mother quarrelled with his wife. In support of his wife's position the son beats his mother. There is a strong belief among the Shona people that beating a parent is taboo. Therefore, a son who beats his mother is bound to never forget that he did something wrong. He will always feel guilty about his wrongdoing. The mother may even die before the matter is rectified, making things worse.

At the same time, when such wrongdoing takes place between a mother and her son, the mother's paternal family is often informed about the incident. The neighbours or some of the village people are bound to know about it. Later in life, each time something goes wrong in the son's life he or other people begin to interpret such misfortunes as punishment for his beating his mother. For example, he may lose his job, be unable to find employment, or simply become desperate or even destitute. All those misfortunes will be attributed to his beating his mother.

The son may go to a traditional healer or for divination to find the cause of his misfortunes in life. The traditional healer often probes tactfully, and might have heard about the incident that his client beat a parent. But often, the healer wants the client to bring it up himself, which often happens. Once the client has admitted the assault, the healer advises the young man to perform a ritual called *kutiza botso*, which means repentance or admitting his wrongdoing.

Often the client will perform the traditional ritual in order to remove the curse. The ritual can be performed whether or not the mother is still living. If the mother is living, the son immediately goes to see his uncle—his mother's brother—and pleads with him for forgiveness and submits himself for the ritual. The uncle will instruct him to put on some old clothes, and stay away from everybody for a week or two weeks. During that time of self-isolation and self-infliction, the son lives as a beggar. He stays out in the bush and eats only what he begs from others.

At some point, the uncle then intervenes by approaching his sister, the mother of the son, and requests that the young man be accepted back as a repentant son. Normally, maternal love immediately prompts the mother to accept the proposal of forgiving her son and reconciling. At that point the mother prepares a meal, most likely with chicken. When the son arrives, his father goes to the *chikuwa* (a raised platform in the traditional kitchen), and either squats or kneels as he offers a prayer of thanksgiving to the ancestors for keeping vigilance over his lost son in his wrongdoing. In such a prayer, the father not only thanks the ancestors, but asks them to convey his thanksgiving to the Creator.

After the father's prayer, the uncle takes charge of the ceremony. He first explains to the two families what happened, and then states his joy at playing the intermediary role between his sister and her son. He announces that he is providing the meat for the meal afterwards. At that point, the son comes into the house where representatives of the two families are gathered. The son has taken a bath that day for the first time after many days of living as a beggar. After he takes his place close to his mother, she takes a morsel of *sadza* (thick porridge food), dips it in soup, and along with a piece of meat gives it to her son as a sign of her forgiveness. As the son graciously receives food from his mother, almost like a little boy again, everybody in the house ululates and claps hands. That means mother and her son are reconciled; the broken relationship between her and her son and between the two families has been restored. Atonement is achieved.

Second, according to Pheko, the Zulus and Babedis of South Africa atoned for those things that did not please God by fasting and keeping away from sinful things. After days of fasting, people gathered at the king's palace and a bull or ox was killed as a sacrifice to God. "It was believed that the animal blood would please God and cause Him to send rain."[6] Or when a girl had a baby before proper marriage, a sheep or goat was killed. Again, it was believed its blood had the power of cleansing her from disgrace (sin), for no man would marry such a woman and even her family was disgraced by her sinful act.[7] Such rituals are familiar in most African ethnic groups on the continent.

Third, Leviticus 16:1–22 lays out what is involved in an atoning ritual: (a) God instructs Aaron through Moses to enter the sanctuary area with a young bull (Lev. 16:3) "for his own sin offering to make atonement for himself and his household" (v. 6), and a ram for a burnt offering (v. 3). (b) Aaron is also instructed to present two goats before the Lord: One goat for the sins of the people is to be slaughtered for a sin offering; the other one is presented live. Then Aaron lays both his hands on the head of the live goat and confesses over it all the wickedness and rebellion of the Israelites and puts them on the goat's head. Finally, Aaron sends away the goat into the desert (vv. 20–22). Thus, the atonement for Israel's sins for that particular year is achieved through the shedding of blood of a bull and a scapegoat that was abandoned in the wilderness bearing the sins of Israel.

Interpretations of the Work of Christ

In the above examples of rituals or acts of atoning for sin among the Shona people of Zimbabwe, the Zulus and Babedis of South Africa, and the Jews in Palestine in Old Testament times, all did what they were humanly able to do to achieve an atonement for sins that estranged families and even the whole community. In Zimbabwe to this day it is not uncommon to see a chicken or goat wandering in the forest—an evidence of a bird or domestic animal that might have been used to atone for some wrongdoing between people or families. People still are searching for atonement.

Christianity has a unique and interesting point concerning atonement: "Whereas most religions believe that man has to do something to atone to God, Christianity teaches that God himself has performed the atoning work. Christianity also teaches that God has performed the sacrifice through Jesus, which has brought God and man back into fellowship with each other."[8]

For instance, Paul wrote, "But God demonstrates his own love for us in this: While we were still sinners, Christ died for us" (Rom. 5:8). Also,

> When you were dead in your sins and in the uncircumcision of your flesh, God made you alive with Christ. He forgave us all our sins, having canceled the charge of our legal indebtedness, which stood against us and condemned us; he has taken it away, nailing it to the cross. And having disarmed the powers and authorities, he made a public spectacle of them, triumphing over them by the cross. (Col. 2:13–15)

And John wrote, "For God so loved the world that he gave his one and only Son, that whoever believes in him shall not perish but have eternal life. For God did not send his Son into the world to condemn the world, but to save the world through him" (John 3:16–17).

The question remains: What exactly did God do for man to be atoned to God? What is the interpretation of the cross as a symbol of atonement? Or what is the efficacy or effectiveness of the Cross of Jesus

Christ to remove sin? According to Vincent Taylor: (a) Jesus believed that his mission was to fulfil the destiny of the Suffering Servant of Isaiah 53 "who bore the sins of many."[9] To that end, he tried to teach his disciples that he was to suffer (Mark 8:31), a point they could not understand until after his crucifixion and the resurrection. (b) He also taught his disciples that he came "to give his life as a ransom for many" (Mark 10:45). Thus, on the night that he was betrayed, he spoke to his disciples of his blood as "shed for many," as surrendered life that should establish a new (covenant) relationship between God and man (Mark 14:24). He also spoke of "the cup" that he had to drink (Mark 10:39, 14:36), and indeed, he suffered the agony of Gethsemane and endured the final desolation of the cross (Mark 15:34).[10]

At the time, Jesus "believed that his suffering, crowned by the victory of the resurrection, was the divinely appointed way by which men might be restored to fellowship with God and made to share in the life of His Kingdom."[11]

Theories Concerning the Efficacy of the Cross

The word *efficacy* means "power to produce intended results; effectiveness." So we need to ask ourselves, why is the cross-resurrection event so central in the Christian faith? How has the church explained how God atoned for humankind through Jesus Christ on the cross? William Hordern points out that while Church Councils were convened on the Trinity and the nature of Christ, there was no such discussion concerning the doctrine of the atonement. Therefore, the church has held three major interpretations of what God did on the cross or cross-resurrection event: the "classic" theory, the Anselmian or satisfactory theory, and the liberal or moral influence theory.

First, *the Ransom or "Classic" Theory of Atonement*. This theory was popular among those in the early church (Matt. 20:28, Mark 10:45, 1 Tim. 2:6, Heb. 9:15), including prominent theologians Irenaeus (c. 115–c. 200),

Origen (c. 185–c. 254), Athanasius (295–373), Augustine (354–430), and Martin Luther (1483–1546).[12]

According to this theory, Satan gained the souls of men to himself because they had sinned. But God made a bargain with Satan, giving him the soul of Jesus even though he did not deserve him, if Satan would release the souls of men who accepted Jesus. That means God gave his only Son to Satan as a ransom for sins committed by all men so that they would be set free. Satan agreed, thinking that Jesus was just a good man. After receiving Jesus, Satan found out that he could not hold or control him, for he was the Son of God. Because the death of Jesus on the cross was inevitably connected to his resurrection through the power of God, Satan ended up with neither the souls that had accepted Christ, nor Christ himself. Satan had been deceived.

There are two problems with this theory. (a) The theory makes God's character questionable—it makes God a deceiver.[13] (b) The theory has also been criticized because it implies that God can buy off the power of Satan.[14]

In spite of the limitations of the ransom or "classic" theory of atonement, the theory teaches two fundamental truths:

(a) It expresses faith that in the death and resurrection of Jesus, God had conquered the forces of evil. God is more powerful than evil.[15] Or,

> the work of atonement is a dramatic struggle between God and the forces of evil in the world. In the incarnate Lord, divinity is deeply hidden. Under the veil of his humanity, Christ battles with the demons, the devil, and all the principalities and powers that hold human beings captive. By his cross and resurrection, Christ decisively defeats these powers and thus frees their captives.[16]

(b) It points to the fact that evil tends to overreach and thus destroy itself. There is a saying that if you give a man enough rope he will hang himself. This is a fact of life. This doctrine was too crude to provide any satisfactory explanation.

Second, *the Objective or Satisfactory or Anselmian theory of Atonement.* Anselm (1033–1109), Archbishop of Canterbury, wrestled with the question, "How can God forgive man's sin?"[17] He argued that man owed obedience to God, the ruler of the universe, but man had failed to obey, violated the trust of God, and hence he fell into debt to God. He had dishonoured God. Therefore, justice demanded either that the debt is paid to God, or that man is punished eternally. Either way would uphold God's prestige as the moral ruler of man. But God did not want to punish man eternally, for God's purpose in creating man was to have fellowship with him. Nor could man give God satisfaction since man already owed perfect obedience and could do no more. If God waved the sin aside and simply forgave, his honour and prestige as ruler would be called into question. We have a dilemma—man owed the debt, but only God could pay it.

So, God sent Jesus, who was both God and man. (a) Because he was God he could pay the debt, and (b) because he was also man he could pay it for man. But even Jesus could not pay it by living a perfect life, for as man, he already owed that to God. But Jesus did not deserve to die since he had not sinned. Consequently, when Jesus gave himself to death, he paid the debt for men. God's honour was vindicated so that he could forgive those who came to him through Christ.

Critics of this theory claim that: (a) "God would not demand the death of an innocent person simply to uphold his own honor and justice."[18] (b) Also, this makes God appear like a feudal landlord who is afraid his serfs might get out of hand if he is too lenient with them.

The most significant thing about the objective or satisfactory or Anselmian theory of atonement is that ". . . it did express the church's belief that forgiveness is not something simple or easy. It cost God to forgive."[19]

Third, *the Subjective, Liberal or Moral Influence Theory of Atonement*. Although younger, Abelard (1079–1142) was a contemporary of Anselm and a critic of his theory. While Anselm's theory may be described as objective, Abelard's theory may be described as a subjective doctrine of atonement. Medieval scholastics favoured this theory. Abelard explains "the Atonement as consisting essentially in a change taking place in men rather than a changed attitude on the part of God."[20] For Abelard, there was nothing on the side of God that made forgiveness impossible. However, forgiveness is a two-way affair. You cannot forgive someone who does not want to be forgiven. Forgiveness is the restoration of broken fellowship, but one cannot restore the fellowship if the other does not wish it be restored. That was God's problem with man, according to Abelard. His theory says there are two critical issues:

(a) God wanted to forgive man, but man wanted to go his own way, merry-making and sinning. Neither did man want to repent or ask for forgiveness. So, at his own initiative, God acted. He sent his Son to suffer and die for man as a manifestation of God's great love. When man sees this he is moved to shame and repents so that God is able to forgive him.

(b) "In the death of Christ we see the love of God in such a way that we are moved to repent."[21]

Hordern says, "Christ's death can only be a revelation of God's love for man if it was a necessary sacrifice." Here is how Isaac Watts articulated that thought, in his hymn, "When I Survey the Wondrous Cross":

> When I survey the wondrous Cross
> On which the Prince of Glory died
> My richest gain I count but loss
> And pour contempt on all my pride

See from his head, his hands his feet
Sorrow and love flow mingled down.
Did e'er such love and sorrow meet
Or thorns compose so rich a crown.[22]

The three theories of atonement, and the New Testament metaphors on which they are based, are not mutually exclusive. Each theory bears a rich contribution toward understanding the work of Christ for our salvation. It may be good to look at their strengths:

1. The strengths of the ransom or "classic theory" are:

(a) In the death and resurrection of Jesus, God conquered the forces of evil and the fear of death, and proved that God is more powerful than evil.

(b) It points to the fact that evil, such as corruption that we see in our communities, government institutions, and in our churches, tends to overreach; and, time and again, we have seen such evil destroying itself. The faithfulness of God and his justice has often had the last word.

2. The objective or satisfactory or Anselmian theory: It did express the church's belief that forgiveness is not something simple or easy. It cost God to forgive, just as it costs a human being his/her pride to receive forgiveness. A story is told of a chief who wanted to eradicate theft among the people of his chieftainship. He enacted a law that any thief caught a second time would have his eyes plucked out. The following day, one of his sons broke the law and was brought before the village council for trial. When the chief was informed what his son had done, instead of breaking his own law by letting his son go free, the chief instructed the council to pluck out one eye of his son and one of his own. The chief forgave his son and instructed him not to do it again for he would then lose both eyes. Indeed, forgiveness is not always easy, whether you forgive or are forgiven you may end up paying a price for it. God, through Jesus Christ, his Son, paid a price for the sin of humanity.

3. The subjective, liberal or moral influence theory: Abelard's theory makes two critical points:

(a) In Christ, God reveals his love for humanity. Coming face to face with God's love in Christ is coming face to face with reality; and that love has changed lives throughout the world.

God wanted to forgive man, but man wanted to go his own way, merry-making and sinning. Neither did he want to repent or ask for forgiveness. So, at his own initiative, God acted. He sent his Son to suffer and die for man as a manifestation of God's great love. When man sees this he is moved to shame and repents so that God is able to forgive him.

(b) One cannot think of Christ on the cross and not be moved to repent. One may ask why Christians choose the cross as a symbol of victory when in the Old Testament it was clear that one hung on a cross was under God's curse (Deut. 21:23), and an issue that drew the attention of Paul to expound on the work of Christ (Gal. 3:13). One will only need to remind oneself of Nelson Mandela's Robin Island prison number 466/64, given to him when he was forty-six years old as he started his twenty-seven year imprisonment[23]; and how, in subsequent years after his release it became a symbol of pride and victory over the evil forces of apartheid. That seems to be what Paul meant by saying, "Christ redeemed us from the curse of the law by becoming a curse for us . . ." (Gal. 3:13). Nelson Mandela became a curse for his people, and for the whole world that had agonized to work to see that evil system of apartheid collapse.

Chapter 10

The Church

James Chikuse was a pastor-teacher in the early days of the United Methodist Church, when it was still known as the Methodist Episcopal Church in Southern Rhodesia. A pastor-teacher was a layperson approved and appointed by the bishop both as a teacher in a school during the week days and as a preacher in one or more local churches during weekends. I am intrigued by Chikuse's excellent understanding of the nature of the church in his context in those early times. I am going to share two of his reports to the Rhodesia Mission Conference of the Methodist Episcopal Church, created in 1901. James Chikuse was appointed by Bishop Joseph Hartzell to serve at Mundenda and Marara stations, about twelve to fifteen kilometres north of Old Mutare Mission in 1915. Let Chikuse speak for himself as he spoke to the first and second sessions of the Rhodesia Mission Conference in English, first in 1916:

> I am very thankful to my God he sent me to Mundenda Station but when I reach there I find no people there stay in God way so I try to find them. I find no church at all for God so I go with boys to cut poles for build church. Now I build nicely church for my God.[1]

Second, in 1917, Chikuse was again invited to share his story about the church at Mundenda and Marara. (NB: The word *boy* or *boys* is given the colonial meaning that refers to an African man or men.)

I trusted my Heavenly Father, who call me to His work in the year 1915. I was appoint to Mundenda and Marara, and when I go there I go just as a shield, and the shield cannot stand by itself, same as I do I can't do any work by my own power.

I teach both morning and afternoon, I also change Sunday by Sunday to each station. I believe yes, God has much power over his people and I trust him because the ten boys give up their hearts to follow Jesus. I was not think when I get there I will see boys do like this. My heart is exceeding delightful to see Bishop has come to Africa. When I was at Marara I call boys together to have meeting all together. I said to them, what is mean to say church, they say to say church is to say teacher. I said No, to say church is you boys you connect yourselves together in Christianity, and I show them two poles which stand between the church to hold the roof, and I say, If this two poles said, I am tired we must go to somewhere can this roof stand? They said No, they will go down. I said what will that do? They say they will break the wall poles and all things and I said, Yes you know that boys, that will break all things. You are the poles of the church, If you get out you will kill your wife and children and mother and father. Stand still like these two poles and I said God told Moses one night, he said to him, Let Joshua go with Israel people tomorrow to frighten the Amalekites, You, Aaron and Hur on the hill lift up the rod. Moses did what God told him. At noon time Moses' hands get tired, he want to put down his hands, and Aaron came to the right hand and Hur to the left hand to support Moses to save his people from dying.

Boys, Do like these two poles. Stand still like Aaron and Hur. Let us come together to-day, we shake hands

> and pray together. After this I call all girls and women together to have their meetings. Joseph Murauro help me to say some things like I say to the boys, and I get up and said to them, you are the wall poles. If you want to get away from God's place you will kill your husband and your children. Do like these two roof poles. They work together to one master. Your Master is Jesus. I have another class at Mundenda. I call all boys together. I said to them, and I said all I been said to the Marara people about two poles stand in the church and Moses and Aaron and Hur lift up the rod to save Israel people. And they confess to sins they had done. After this I trust to my Heavenly Father about his power and love.[2]

The Kingdom of God and the Church

There is often confusion concerning the kingdom of God and the church, and essentially, there is more of a relationship between the two than there are differences. First, *the kingdom of God*: The Greek word *basileia* denotes sovereignty, royal power, and dominion (Rev. 17:18). This word is often used of the kingdom of God or Christ to refer to the sphere of God's rule (Ps. 22:28, Luke 1:33, Rom. 13:1–2).[3] There is widespread agreement that the primary meaning of the word *basileia* is kingly rule, kingship, or sovereignty—not kingdom, as if to suggest a territory governed.[4] Therefore, one can talk of God's rule or God's sovereignty on earth, in spite of the existence of human kingdoms. The New Testament "*basileia* is the whole new activity of God which is proceeding in the life and work of Jesus."[5] It is indeed the new order that Jesus announces: "The time has come . . . The kingdom of God has come near. Repent and believe the good news!" (Mark 1:15). That means even if the earthly kings set themselves against God's kingdom or will, God will still have the last word.[6] Harold DeWolf defines the kingdom of God as "the reign of God, the realm in which His will is done 'as it is in heaven'."[7] Jesus embraces that kingdom; and partly, he fulfilled the expectation of the life of the kingdom of God through his ministry of curing many who had diseases, sickness, and evil spirits, and giving sight to many who were blind (Luke 7:20–23).

Second, *the church*: The word *church* does not occur in the Old Testament. However, in the Septuagint version, the words *congregation* and *assembly* are translated *ecclesia*, meaning the people of God. In the Old Testament the concept of congregation is traced back to the people of Israel, who were considered as a group for travel (Exod. 16:1) or worship (Isa. 1:12–13).[8] The Exodus idea, "a group for travel," is often shared in the United Methodist Church in Zimbabwe circles as "*tiriparwendo*," meaning we are on a journey or on the pilgrimage of faith. That means "behind the word church as we know it in Christianity, lies the ancient concept, deep rooted in the Old Testament, of a chosen people of God, both ideally regarded and actually called out in solemn assembly."[9] That is the story of the *Old Covenant*—God and the people of Israel.

The church is an assembly or congregation of people called together by God for a purpose. It is indeed, ". . . the object of divine activity, and then the organ or instrument of God's purpose for mankind"[10] to continue the work of Christ on earth. In the New Testament the Greek word *ecclesia* (*ek-lay-see-ah*) means an assembly (Acts 19:32)—a local congregation (Matt. 18:17) or the church universal (16:18).[11] That is what James Chikuse did not see when he was appointed to Mundenda in 1915: "I find no people there stay in God way." But thanks to God for what happened later, as he says, "God has much power over his people and I trust him because the ten boys give up their hearts to follow Jesus." In other words, ten converts had been won to Christ; and at that point there was the church of Christ. When Chikuse was at Marara, those were the people he exhorted "to say church is you boys you connect yourselves together in Christianity . . ."

The Teaching of Jesus on the Church

The word *ecclesia* is found only twice in the Gospels (Matt. 16:18, 18:17). This has led to a debate, with some doubting whether Jesus used the word *ecclesia* or its equivalent in Aramaic. Other scholars, however, say even if Jesus did not use the word, his mission was the formation of a new people of God. Although the expression "new Israel" may not be in the New Testament, "the idea of the Christian community as having now become 'the new Israel of God'" does appear: (a) "Peace and mercy to all who follow this rule—to the Israel of God" (Gal. 6:16), (b) Compare, "Understand, then, that those *who* have faith are children of Abraham" (Gal. 3:7), "All nations will be blessed through you" (Gal 3:8), and "If you belong to Christ, then you are Abraham's seed, and heirs according to the promise" (Gal. 3: 29). The expression is made "in many ways."[12] If Jesus did not use the word *ecclesia*, the evidence can be summarized as follows:

First, the kingdom that lies at the heart of Jesus' message implied a "new people of God." While the Jews expected one to come in the distant future, Jesus says the hour is now; it is happening now. So he called some disciples to follow him, and to live under the rule of God[13]—showing it was the dawn of a new era.

Second, Jesus thought of himself in terms of Isaiah's Servant of Yahweh in the Old Testament, quoted in Matthew 12:18–21. In Isaiah, the "Servant" Messiah (which referred to a community) became through his suffering the creator of a new people of God (Isa. 42:1–4, 49:1–7, 50:4–9, 52:13–53:12).[14]

Third, when Jesus talked of being a shepherd and his disciples a flock, he described his messianic task of gathering the people of God (Ezek. 34:12, 16, 23, Mic. 5:2–4). Jesus is the shepherd sent to the lost sheep of Israel (Matt. 10:6)—all the lost sheep (Luke 15:3–7).[15]

Fourth, the preaching and teaching of Jesus were completed by his actions. (a) He called, appointed, and designated the twelve apostles—representing the twelve tribes of Israel (Mark. 3:13–19); and created "a new Israel, a new People of God, a new church; although it was the re-creation of the one which existed in Israel, and went back ultimately to the original purpose of God, who chose Israel as the instrument of His revelation."[16] (b) Jesus' Sermon on the Mount (Matt. 5–7) is a convenient summary of his teaching to his disciples.[17] (c) Jesus sent out his disciples on a mission. He sent out the Twelve (Matt. 12:5), and the seventy-two (Luke 10:1–2). (d) Jesus established a covenant with his disciples: "This is my blood of the covenant, which is poured out for many . . . (Mark 14:24). In 1 Corinthians, we find Paul's version: "This cup is the new covenant in my blood; do this, whenever you drink it, in remembrance of me (1 Cor. 11:25). "The Israel of the Old Testament was a covenant people; now Jesus, speaking to the Twelve as representatives of the church as a whole, establishes a new covenant with them, the new Israel of God—and yet not unrelated to the old."[18]

The Church of Easter and Pentecost

Gustaf Aulen says, "The Christian church is the church of Easter and Pentecost."[19] First, it is the church of Easter for the following reasons: (a) It was the resurrection of Jesus that illuminated the whole *kerygma* (as cited by C. H. Dodd): (i) that is, the resurrection illuminated what Jesus had done in the past, the age of fulfilment that had dawned, his ministry, teaching and preaching, his suffering and his death, and so the gospel was preached backward; (ii) the resurrection illuminated what was to happen in the present-future: his exaltation at the right hand of God as the messianic head of the new Israel, the coming of the Holy Spirit in his church as sign of Christ's present power and glory, the Messianic Age that will soon reach its consummation in the return of Christ; and (iii) the sharing of this message of the resurrection of Jesus Christ must always end with an appeal for repentance and baptism in Jesus' name, and the offer of forgiveness of sins and the gift of the Holy Spirit.[20] Eventually, the gospel was preached backward to Jesus' birth.

(b) The Christian church is the church of Easter because it "is the result of the finished work of Christ."[21] When Jesus uttered the words from the cross "It is finished" (John 19:30), he had through his teaching, preaching, ministry, and sacrificial life finished laying out the foundation of his church. He never feared death, for even in its face Jesus saw his trusting Father. Hence, he said, "Father, into your hands I commit my spirit" (Luke 23:46). Thus Jesus Christ became the "precious stone for a sure foundation" (Isa. 28:16), of which Paul says, "For no one can lay any foundation other than the one already laid, which is Jesus Christ" (1 Cor. 3:11).

(c) The Christian church is the church of Easter because the resurrection of Jesus became the pivotal message of the disciples of Jesus—the message from which all the finished work of Jesus made sense. Paul argued systematically and vigorously in supporting the resurrection of the dead by basing it on Christ who was raised historically on the third day (1 Cor. 15:4). He had evidence of the risen Christ—who appeared historically to Peter, to the Twelve, to more than five hundred, most of whom were still present [and could be interviewed], to James, and lastly to Paul himself (1 Cor. 15:4–8). Paul went on to say that if Christ had not been raised, the consequences to the Christian enterprise would be disastrous: (i) Christian preaching is useless, and so is your faith (1 Cor. 15:14), (ii) Christians would be false witnesses about God (1 Cor. 15:15), (iii) the dead would not be raised (1 Cor. 15:16), and (iv) your faith is futile and you are still in your sins (1 Cor. 15:17). No wonder the first good news of the Christian faith on that Easter Sunday morning was "He is risen!" (Mark 16:6, Matt. 28:6, Luke 24:6). From the message of the resurrection of Jesus the whole gospel found its illumination, credibility, authenticity, and vindication. Without the resurrection of Jesus from the dead, the cross, his teaching and preaching, and his ministry of healing would have come to nothing. Thank God, the message of the Easter Sunday that morning rang out: "He is risen! He is risen!" The whole gospel of Jesus Christ was preached backward—beginning with the resurrection to the cross, his preaching, teaching and healing, and even to his origin.

(d) The Christian church is the church of Easter because: (i) in the resurrection of Jesus believers find and experience *victory over the powers of evil and sin*, and (ii) in the resurrection of Jesus we experience victory over the fear of death, witchcraft, and all types of political demagogues. Indeed, Paul cries out, "Where, O death is your victory? Where, O death is your sting?" (1 Cor. 15:55). The message of victory is at the same time the message of hope. No other message communicates hope to humankind than the resurrection of Jesus Christ. Thus in celebrating the gospel Paul says, "No, in all these things we are more than conquerors through him who loved us" (Rom. 8:37).

Second, the Christian church is the church of Pentecost. (a) It is the church of Pentecost because *it was born on the day of Pentecost*—on 28 May 30 CE.[22] Pentecost became the day of fulfilment of the promise of Jesus, who had long pledged to his disciples the *power* of the Holy Spirit, when he said, ". . . but stay in the city until you have been clothed with power from on high" (Luke 24:49), and, "you will receive power when the Holy Spirit comes on you; and you will be my witnesses in Jerusalem, and in all Judea and Samaria, and to the ends of the earth" (Acts 1:8). (b) The Christian church is the church of Pentecost because it was born in the power of the Holy Spirit. "When the day of Pentecost came, they were all together in one place . . . All of them were filled with the Holy Spirit . . ." (Acts 2:1–4).

(c) The Christian church is the church of Pentecost because at the occasion of its birth on the day of Pentecost the Holy Spirit, the Giver of life, served as the midwife. Not only were the disciples in the upper room filled with the Holy Spirit; on that same day, Peter proclaimed Christ, and three thousand converts received forgiveness of sin and the gift of the Holy Spirit (Acts 2:36–37).

(d) "The filling with the Spirit was an experience to be repeated on several occasions (Acts 4:8, 31, 13:9); but the Spirit-baptism took place once and for all, so far as the believing community was concerned."[23] Pentecost was essentially "a community experience, deeply personal, and yet not individualistic."[24]

Nature of the Church

First, the church is the dominion of Christ on earth. A dominion is a ruled or governed territory or country. So Christ rules the church. It is so because the church is the finished work of Christ; Christ is the foundation of his church. In this church Jesus calls people from all backgrounds into a new community, where there is "neither Jew nor Gentile, neither slave nor free, nor is there male and female, for you are all one in Christ Jesus" (Gal. 3:28).

Second, the church and Christ belong together. Christ and his church are inseparable. The church is "the body of Christ," and at the same time, Christ is the head of that body (Col. 1:18); Jesus is the vine, and the disciples are the branches (John 15:5).

Third, the church is *koinonia* (fellowship). The Greek word *koinonia* in the New Testament means fellowship, a close mutual relationship, participation, sharing in partnership, contribution, or gift. While the church is the finished work of Christ, it is also a *koinonia* created by the Holy Spirit. The early church in Jerusalem was known for how members were connected to and concerned for one another. In their fellowship, they devoted themselves to the teaching of the apostles, to breaking bread, and to praying together in their homes (Acts 2:42), as well as to sharing their possessions (Acts 5:32ff).

Fourth, the church is a missionary community. The God that Christians worship is the missionary God, and his Son, Jesus Christ, expressed this truth in the Great Commission in a number of ways: (a) "As the Father has sent me, I am sending you" (John 20:21), (b) "Therefore go and make disciples of all nations . . ." (Matt. 28:19), (c) "Go into all the world and preach the gospel to all creation" (Mark 16:15), and (d) "Peace be with you" (Luke 24:36).

Fifth, the church of Christ has its distinctive marks. Marks of the church have been cited as *unity, apostolicity,* and *ecumenicity* or *catholicism.* (a) Since the church is the dominion of Christ, and since it has one Lord, there is only *one* church. (b) "The church is called apostolic because the gospel by which the church is built was given to it as an apostolic message, and because this message is continually proclaimed anew by other messengers following in the footsteps of the apostles."[25] (c) In spite of the church schism that came through the accident of history, Eastern and Western (or Byzantine and Roman) Catholicism in the eleventh century, Roman Catholicism and European Reformation in the sixteenth century and the nineteenth century, both the finished work and the continuing work of Christ are universal in character.[26] The Greek word that expresses the fact of the range of the church's fellowship satisfactorily is *oikoumene,* meaning "the whole inhabited world."[27]

Major Concepts of the Church

First, the Orthodox Church (Greek, Russian, Serbian, etc.) holds that it alone maintains the full teaching, tradition, and order of the "one true and visible Church of Christ on earth." This is not considered by the Orthodox to be an arrogant assertion, but an honest confession of faith and appeal to history. Other Christian bodies are not dismissed as being heretical, but are adjudged to lack the requisite fullness. Of course, this is similar to the teaching of the Roman Catholic Church about itself, except that the papacy is believed by Roman Catholics to be indispensable.

Second, the Old Catholic Church of Europe, the Polish National Catholic Church (largely in America), and the churches of the Anglican Communion likewise believe that they have maintained the pure Christian teaching, the proper ministry in apostolic Episcopal succession, and the true sacraments. While recognizing the integrity and validity of other Episcopal communions, these churches usually regard the non-Episcopal churches as being not false but deficient.

Third, Lutheran churches have a clear statement in the Augsburg Confession to the effect that the church "is the congregation of believers, where the Gospel is purely preached and the Sacraments rightly administered." Forms of ministry and order are secondary, even though some, such as Scandinavian churches, have bishops. Lutherans generally permit full sacramental fellowship at "pulpit and altar" only with those who agree with them on the meaning and interpretation of the Gospel and the sacraments.

Fourth, the Reformed or Presbyterian Churches also teach that the word of God (the Gospel) and the sacraments are the essentials that make a congregation a Christian church, but they add the necessity of an order of discipline.

Fifth, the Methodists, being derived historically from the Church of England and influenced by the Reformed, have a comprehensive doctrine of the church that permits them to recognize readily and fully most other Christian communions.

Sixth, Congregationalists hold the distinctive view that the local congregation is the essential and autonomous unit of the church. Congregations in covenant and fellowship with one another constitute the whole church.

Seventh, Baptists and Disciples of Christ are also congregational in polity, but lay down the added requirement that only persons baptized as believers, rather than as infants, may be members of the church. Many such churches require baptism by total immersion as being in accord with the New Testament practice.

Eighth, the Society of Friends (Quakers) witness to a Christian fellowship independent of creeds, orders, and sacraments.

Ninth, various other denominations find their views of the church expressed in one or more of the above categories. In recent years there have come into being by mergers a number of United Churches, combining distinct elements of their constituent bodies. Only the Church of South India has united churches of Episcopal, Presbyteral, and

Congregational ministries, although such an attempt is being made in several countries. The force of the contemporary ecumenical movement lies not in its insistence that denominations should merge according to a common pattern, but that they seek freely in their particular circumstances to overcome divisive barriers, to renew the corporate life and services of the churches, and to find effective means for extending the Christian mission to all persons.[28]

Chapter 11

The Church and God's Mission

The word *mission* comes from the Latin word *missio*, meaning a sending or being sent away to perform a special duty. We often talk of a person being on a special mission. Denominational churches send out missionaries in their own countries and to foreign countries. We need to remember that the church may have its own mission, but authentically what the church should do is carry out God's mission. This is what Jesus meant when he instructed his disciples, "As the Father has sent me, I am sending you" (John 20:21).

Being sent out by Jesus was not a new thing for the disciples, for there were other occasions when Jesus had sent them in twos (Matt. 10:1ff, Mark 6:6ff, Luke 10:1ff). Neither did the risen Christ Jesus sending out the disciples into the world mean the disciples were taking the place of Jesus, for Jesus had specifically instructed his disciples earlier on concerning who would take his place when he was gone. It was not his plan to leave them as orphans (John 14:18). He told them, "If you love me, keep my commands. And I will ask the Father, and he will give you another advocate to help you and be with you forever—the Spirit of truth" (John 14:15–17). Thus, it was the Holy Spirit who took over the place of Jesus and continued leading the church in the mission of God that Jesus had launched into the world. The question that we may raise is: Under the guidance of the Holy Spirit, what does the church discern as God's mission in the world? Or what does the African church discern as God's mission on the continent of Africa? As much as the thought is overwhelming, one has to start somewhere.

The Worshipping Church

The church's worship of God every Sunday is the first and greatest mark of a church that is led by the Holy Spirit to continue the work of Christ. The Gospel of Matthew tells the story of the visit of the Wise Men or Magi from the East to Bethlehem. After seeing his star, they travelled there looking for the baby Jesus so that they could worship him. When they finally saw the child with his mother, Mary, ". . . they bowed down and worshiped him" (Matt. 2:11), and thereafter, they presented him with gifts. Similarly, when the eleven disciples met the risen Christ in Galilee at a mountain where they had been directed, almost instantly "they worshiped him," although some still had doubts (Matt. 28:17). Some doubted as they saw him from afar, but as the Christ drew nearer them, they were confronted by the truth—the reality of his resurrection—as death had stripped him of those bonds of time and space that tie all men and women to this earth.[1]

The expectations of people planning to attend a worship service are innumerable—some are noble and others ignoble. Some of the expectations we will never know. But thank God, some of those expectations are captured in the Order of Sunday Worship.

Let us look at a few of those items in the Order of Worship of the United Methodist Church. First, the *call to worship*. A call to worship is an occasion to alert and simultaneously invite the congregation to begin offering their worship to God. In Zimbabwe, among the Manyika of the Shona people, when a gathering realizes the presence of their chief, an announcement is made: "N*gatikwidze mawoko kuna* Mambo *or* Ishe," meaning, let us ascend or raise our hands to the chief; or let us praise the chief by clapping our hands together. At this announcement all other conversations stop. Words of greeting and praising are uttered simultaneously with men clapping hands first, followed by the women, who clap hands in their own way and ululate at the same time. That way of recognition of the chief by a gathering is a sign that whatever business is to be discussed or carried out has already begun. It also implies that all have turned their minds away from everything else, and are ready to hear from the chief. From Nigerian films we learn that the attention of people before the chief is captured by a greeting, *Igwe---e*!

Second, the *first congregational hymn*. A call to worship is followed by a powerful congregational hymn, such as "M'*tsvene*, M'*tsvene*, M'*tsvene*" ("Holy, Holy, Holy"). As much as I love choir singing, asking the congregation to sit down so the choir can sing first is quenching the Spirit (1 Thess. 5:19). The call to worship should be immediately followed by a congregational hymn of praise and thanksgiving. This is the time when God must hear the voices of all his children who have gathered to offer their worship to him. That first hymn may influence whether visitors want to return. The church should sing with joy, hope, and great expectation.

Third, *the affirmation of faith*. The singing of a great opening hymn is often followed by the affirmation of faith: "I believe in God the Father Almighty, maker of heaven and earth . . . And in Jesus Christ, his only Son our Lord . . . I believe in the Holy Spirit, the holy catholic church, the communion of saints . . ." As the affirmation is a proclamation of the gospel, one may wish that the congregation would speak it slowly enough to make it meaningful. As we declare the affirmation of faith every Sunday in worship, we are speaking of what we have experienced in our own lives, and that we believe what we say.

Fourth, *the pastoral prayer*. This prayer is the monopoly of the pastor for he/she alone carries the burden of the flock—members and people of the community. The prayer is characterized by the following elements: (a) adoration—recognition of God as God, (b) invocation—calling upon God to assist us in our worship (Rom. 8:26), (c) confession—repentance in order to be renewed, (d) thanksgiving—response to the gospel of God's grace, (e) supplication—prayer for our own needs, and (f) intercession—prayer to God for other people's needs, including the sick, the bereaved, those in the community who are troubled, and all society. People often feel their burdens rolled away when they hear the pastor praying for their particular problems. Avoid using singular pronouns in the prayer—"Lord, I pray to you"—because a believer never prays alone. It is good for each member of a local church to know that when he/she prays at home for something, especially in the church or community, there may be another ten or twenty members who are praying to God about the same issue. Prayer is corporate, so use plural pronouns—"We pray to you"—for we are often many united in prayer. Such understanding of prayer binds the church of Christ together.

Fifth, *choir singing*. The role of the choir is to lead the whole church in congregational singing, not to stage a concert that reduces the congregation to spectators. The choir certainly has its place in the order of worship and a good choir can be a blessing to a local church, for it meets expectations of many worshippers. Sixth, *Bible reading*. Attend to the reading of the Bible in the early stages of the Order of Service, reading a text from the Old Testament and another from the New Testament. Others may read one scripture from the Old Testament, another from the Letters, and the last from the Gospels. Bible readers should be told well in advance so that they have time to rehearse their reading, for good reading amounts to proclamation itself.

Seventh, *announcements*. Church announcements should be kept short, to prevent lay leaders from telling stories as if they are preaching. If possible, print out the Order of Worship as well as important announcements.

Eighth, *preaching*. Preaching is central to Sunday worship. Everything in the worship order leads to the time when the Word is proclaimed; whatever comes after must not distort the Word preached. Good preaching focuses on the gospel—preaching Christ contextually in relation to the situation of the people. Avoid using the pulpit as a place to attack other people or one's enemies. Often, long sermons are a result of an unprepared sermon from an unprepared preacher.

One cannot prescribe a worship pattern for all local churches, but if each of the above parts of worship is done timely, the Sunday morning service will attract a significant number of worshippers, even for the first time. Gone are the days when a preacher would stand in the pulpit and say, "In Africa the sun never sets." It does set. Or, "In Africa we do not have to worry about time." People do worry about time nowadays, especially when there is a football game taking place that afternoon. Neither should we view those who attend soccer games on Sunday as less spiritual than the so-called "committed ones." That may not be true any more. Good preaching delivers the message of the day, urgently and passionately, and thereafter the preacher sits down.

The Praying Church

Prayer is a great mark of a church that is led by the Holy Spirit to continue with the work of Christ. The church in Africa is known as a praying church.

First, there are two definitions of prayer that may be helpful. (a) While in seminary, I attended a workshop led by two professors on the subject of prayer. One of the professors, George Buttrick, said, "Prayer is conversation with God." That sounded so profound to me that the more I thought about it, the more I have come to appreciate that understanding of prayer in my personal life. Actually, Jesus taught his disciples to pray as conversation with the Father:

> Our Father in heaven!
> May your name be kept holy.
> May your kingdom come,
> Your will be done on earth as in heaven.
>
> Give us the food we need today.
> Forgive us what we have done wrong,
> As we too forgive those who have wronged us.

And do not lead us into hard testing,
But keep us safe from the Evil One.
For kingship, power and glory are yours forever.
(Matt. 6:6–13)[2]

A Christian who regards himself/herself as a child of God has access to God as Father, and may ask him for all these things. And God hears and responds to those requests, as Jesus taught his disciples. But he may not always respond the way we expect or want, as he said through the prophet Isaiah: "For my thoughts are not your thoughts, neither are your ways my ways . . . As the heavens are higher than the earth, so are my ways higher than your ways and my thoughts than your thoughts" (Isa. 55:8–9).

Further, when we ask for anything from God, we do not tell him what to do. We simply present our request or express our need, which he may already know. Paul shares an agonizing experience he had with the Christians in Corinth in his letter to them. He says, ". . . I was given a thorn in my flesh, a messenger of Satan, to torment me. Three times I pleaded with the Lord to take it away from me. But he said to me, 'My grace is sufficient for you, for my power is made perfect in weakness'" (2 Cor. 12:7–9). That means the Lord heard Paul's plea and he answered. But God answered Paul in a way the latter might not have thought of—that a better solution than to remove Paul's thorn was to teach Paul that human weakness provides the ideal opportunity for the display of divine power (Eph. 3:16, Phil. 4:13).[3] Yes, prayer is conversation with God.

(b) Later on in my life of study, I came across a book by Oscar Cullmann, who defined prayer in another way: "Praying is at the same time both the greatest gift of grace vouchsafed [to be gracious enough] to us, and a difficult task which has to be learned."[4] (i) "The greatest gift of grace vouchsafed to us": I interpret this to mean the indwelling Spirit nudges a believer or believers to pray; and when one finally gets to pray, one is responding to the urge of the Spirit to pray. Or a group of believers may be moved to pray. When we believed, we also received the Spirit of sonship or daughtership to God (Rom. 8:15). There are times when we do not know what to pray for, and Paul rightly says, "But the Spirit himself intercedes for us through wordless groans" (Rom. 8:26). (ii) ". . . and a difficult task which has to be learned": There is a great need for believers to learn to pray. We may not always feel the urge to pray; thus we need to have a disciplined prayer life. It is not easy, and that is why one of the disciples of Jesus after observing the prayer life of the Master said to Jesus, "Lord, teach us to pray, just as John taught his disciples" (Luke 11:1). Prayerful life is a gift, but also a difficult task that the church needs to do always, for prayerful life sustains a warm relationship in conversation with our Father.

Second, there is need for the church to learn from Jesus how to pray; for Jesus actually lived the exemplary life of prayer. There are several occasions when Jesus is observed praying in the Gospels. Often he prayed in solitary places (Mark 1:35, Luke 4:42), and of course in Gethsemane (Mark 14:35, Matt. 26:39, Luke 22:41). It is important to study together as the church or groups of the church what Jesus taught about prayer (Matt. 6:5–12) and the parable of the Pharisee and the Tax Collector (Luke 18:9–14).

Prayer is a corporate conversation. As believers we understand that no one ever prays alone. Elijah learned that lesson when he thought he was the only one left (1 Kings 19:14), only to learn that there were "seven thousand in Israel whose knees have not bowed down to Baal and all whose mouths have not kissed him" (1 Kings 19:18). Even when you kneel down as an individual, you are not alone in prayer. Many Christians in a family pray for each other; many Christians in a local church pray for their fellow members; many Christians in a nation pray for their leaders; and many Christians pray for those falsely accused for misdeeds. If we think of prayer that way, we begin to realize that prayer is a great spiritual gift or force given to believers. Indeed, prayer is a corporate ministry to Christians. We intercede for others, even those that we do not know.

Third, churches need to encourage prayer cells. William Sangster, a distinguished Methodist preacher in England in the 1950s, proposed four types of prayer cells that can be established in a local church: (a) Family Prayer Cell—where families are encouraged to engage in regular prayers at their own convenient time. Indeed, if there is a time and place where people learn to pray, it is as children in family prayers. Even when children are no longer at home, they always know that Dad and Mum at home are praying for each one of them by name. It is also in such family prayers that children learn to pray for one another, and pray for their parents. Family prayers are the most appropriate arena for prayer training. My own father and mother were persons of prayer who led us in prayer every evening after supper. (b) Business Prayer Cell—where business groups of men or women meet at a convenient time, either for breakfast (in urban areas) or for a cup of tea in homes (especially for women), focusing their time together on prayer. (c) Neighbourhood Prayer Cell—where prayer groups meet not only in the homes of believers but also in the homes of seekers who may extend an invitation for such prayers in their homes. (d) Church Prayer Cell—where local church members may be praying for a special event, such as praying for rain, praying for a revival meeting, praying for the young people of the community, or praying for peace during an upcoming election event.[5]

The Evangelistic Preaching Church

A church that is led by the Holy Spirit to continue with the work of Christ on earth pays attention to evangelistic preaching.

First, *the pulpit must lift Christ*: "Just as Moses lifted up the snake in the wilderness, so the Son of Man must be lifted up, that everyone who believes may have eternal life in him" (John 3:14–15). No matter if one preaches a biblical sermon, doctrinal sermon, or life situation sermon, ultimately Christ must be lifted in such a way that the listeners may decide for themselves to follow him. Today, many African urban churches are overwhelmed by young people who are searching for something meaningful in life. As we proclaim Christ, the Holy Spirit will do his work to convict people to live the kind of life that they may be searching for.

Second, *proclaim the promises of God in the Bible*: Our preachers, clergy or laity, must learn to unpack biblical promises that are pregnant with what God can do for his people. Listen to a few of the promises that are in the scriptures: (a) "What is that in your hand?" (Exod. 4:2). (b) "For I know plans I have for you . . . plans to prosper you and not to harm you, plans to give you hope and a future" (Jer. 29:11). (c) "Ask and it will be given to you; seek and you will find; knock and the door will be opened to you" (Matt. 7:7). (d) "Come to me, all you who are weary and burdened, and I will give you rest" (Matt. 11:28). (e) "Here I am! I stand at the door and knock. If anyone hears my voice and opens the door, I will come in and eat with that person, and they with me" (Rev. 3:20). This is only part of an inexhaustible range of divine promises for exposition—divine promises pregnant with the gracious evangelistic message of God through his Son.

Third, *the altar call*: William Sangster made a significant point when he wrote, "Where the evangelical appeal is rarely or never sounded, an awful incompleteness hangs over the whole work."[6] A church that wants to continue with the work of Christ, especially in Africa, needs to learn to be comfortable with extending an invitation or altar call. The biblical background and theological rationale for the practice of an altar call is as follows: "The altar-call is an invitation to Christian discipleship."[7] It is an appeal to make a public commitment to Christ by individuals who have not done so. It is an encouragement to persons who might want to make a commitment or to start their life all over—call it a re-dedication or another beginning. Often people want to express their response to the gospel after proclamation. John the Baptist used an altar call (Luke 3:1–14); Peter used it on the day of Pentecost (Acts 2:37).

The Bible-studying Church

A Bible-studying church is a church that continues with the work of Christ, led by the Holy Spirit in its community. In November 2010, American management expert Stephen Covey spoke in Harare on the topic "The Art of Leadership and Its Impact on Organizational Success." In his speech he pointed out that companies and institutions needed to realize that the world was moving from an Industrial Age to a Knowledge Worker Age, where we have to recognize that every one of us is born with magnificent gifts, talents, capacities, privileges, intelligences, and opportunities with infinite potential. He also advocated for high-trust leadership where control is substituted with empowerment, because most organizations possess employees sitting on immense talent that is just waiting to be unlocked.[8]

About 55 and 57 CE, Paul wrote about the early church as one body—the body of Christ, composed of a people with a diversity of spiritual gifts (1 Cor. 12:1–13) and different gifts (Rom. 12:1–8) respectively. Those spiritual gifts that are endowed in us are often realized when we become concerned with our lives or are in search for purposeful meaning to our lives and the world at large. Needless to say conversion of one's life to Christ has often provided fulfilment in the search for purposeful living and a new destiny in life. Reading and studying the Bible has often provided that turning point to a new realization for individual Christians.

An example is Augustine, who suffered from self-disgust because of his inability to control his sexual desires. At the height of his struggle he fled from his friends and went into a garden where he felt he heard the voice of a child commanding him to "take and read." Having a copy of Paul's letter to the Romans, his eyes fell on the passage in the thirteenth chapter that included the following: "Let us behave decently, as in the daytime, not in carousing and drunkenness, not in sexual immorality and debauchery, not in dissension and jealousy. Rather, clothe yourselves with the Lord Jesus Christ, and do not think about how to gratify the desires of the flesh" (Rom. 13:13–14).

Augustine's act of obeying the voice of a child and reading Paul's letter to the Romans transformed his whole life and utilized his great intellectual powers as Bishop of Hippo, and a great leader of the church.

The major reason we read and study the Bible is religious,[9] and one of the great achievements of the Bible Society has been to make the Bible available in the vernacular languages of as many peoples on earth as possible. In our African local churches there are persons who have no access to any other book to read than the Bible. Such persons read their Bible almost on a daily basis, but they do not always understand what they read (Acts 8:30f). This episode of the Ethiopian eunuch and Philip presents a challenge to preachers, whether they are clergy or laity. The Bible needs explanation.

Our local churches are packed with individual members endowed with hundreds of gifts or talents that the church as an institution is sitting on, primarily because of the church's traditional style that emphasizes control instead of empowerment. Bible study empowers the laity to use their God-given gifts to build up the church. The church needs to recognize people's various gifts and talents and help them achieve the infinite potential of their lives and that of the mission of the church. For that to happen, every local church would need to have a viable Bible study programme as part of its mission. Bible study unlocks unspeakable realization of talents and gifts that the local church may possess. A local church may need to follow the following guidelines:

First, the pastor should train laity who may be interested to lead Bible study groups either at the church, at class meetings, or in the sections. The groups should not be forced on people, but there are always several people in every local church who want to study the Bible. Often, the problem is finding someone to teach them. Although *class meetings* in the Methodist Societies in England originated as a way of raising funds for the rebuilding of a Society New Room in Bristol, eventually they developed into a unit of Society membership (12 members), and the training ground for lay leaders, who became a strong instrument of evangelism and Christian education.[10] The introduction and training of the laity in preaching, teaching, and participating in the leadership of propagating the gospel was the genius of the Methodist Revival of the eighteenth century.

Second, the venue for Bible study is determined by the situation in which a local church is located. Bible study groups can meet at the church, in the homes of church members, or anywhere else convenient for people.

Third, Bible study can also be emphasized in any number of special groups, including confirmation or initiation classes, church organization groups such as Women's Organization, Men's Organization, and Youth, church choir retreats, and other church groups.

Fourth, there are several advantages that come with Bible study: (a) Bible study brings about the *spirit of renewal* in the local church (2 Kings 22:8, Acts 1:1–6:7, 6:8–9:31, 9:32–12:24). (b) Bible study reinforces *the spirit of confidence in reading our Bibles*. Many members read the Bible alone at home, and live with unanswered questions in their effort to study the Bible. (c) An effective Bible study programme unlocks those gifts, talents, capacities, and opportunities for people so that they grow toward the realization of their potential. (d) The Bible is not just about "spiritual" things; it is also about talents (Matt. 25:14–30), gifts (1 Cor. 12:4–11), and health care and healing (Mark 1:30, 2:1–5, Acts 3:1–10, 1 Tim. 5:23). (e) Through Bible study, we can be transformed intellectually, socially, and spiritually as we are inspired and challenged "to know and experience God through Jesus Christ, claim and live God's promises, and grow and serve as Christian disciples."[11]

The Fellowship (*Koinonia*) and Caring Church

The local church can be described and understood best as the *koinonia*—the fellowship or the communion God has with all his saints—and communion among the saints themselves, the faithful ones to the Lord. It can also be described as a caring church in the community.

First, the church as a fellowship church: In his first letter to the church in Corinth (1 Cor. 11:17ff), Paul writes about the early church in fellowship; and that fellowship was divided in two parts or two meals that took place in the church: (a) There was the ordinary meal or supper, to which members of the church brought food from their homes. We call it potluck. Those who had more food were encouraged to bring more food, not just for themselves, but for the sake of the poor. All shared their resources, and no one was left out or went home hungry. (b) The ordinary meal was followed by the Eucharist, where everyone again participated together. Paul cautioned members of the Corinthian church about the Eucharist: "Is not the cup of thanksgiving for which we give thanks a participation in the blood of Christ? And is not the bread we break a participation in the body of Christ? Because there is one loaf, we, who are many, are one body, for we all share the one loaf" (1 Cor. 10:16–17).

Time and again, the local church as a fellowship is supposed to come together, in spite of divisions that may occur. The church gains more in their various ministries in the community by promoting fellowship than when it becomes an agent of disunity. In Africa, many of our communities fall victim to disunity caused by tribalism, party politics, denominationalism, and many others. There is a need for the church to demonstrate itself as an inclusive community for a broken and divided Africa. The church can express this fellowship in a number of ways:

(a) Testimonies as a way of fellowship: On the second day of the first session of the East Central Africa Mission Conference, 17 November 1901, Bishop Hartzell led the "Love-feast" service at St. Andrew's Methodist Episcopal Church, Mutare, Southern Rhodesia, where participants shared testimonies. That practice, started over a hundred years ago in Zimbabwe, has stayed with us to this day. Testimonies are an enriching celebration of Christian fellowship in Methodism throughout Africa. Terence Ranger, who was professor of race relations and

Chair of the African Studies Committee at the University of Oxford, made this observation about African United Methodist testimonies:

> African Christian testimonies—made use of and interpreted in all these ways—constituted a major genre of both official and popular Methodism in eastern Zimbabwe and Mozambique. Nothing similar survives for eastern Zimbabwean Catholicism and Anglicanism. AMEC [American Methodist Episcopal Church] missionaries not only had a particular interest in testimonies, they also had a particular interest in sermons.[12]

(b) Hymn singing: How wonderful it is when a local church finds ways to meet regularly for hymn singing. Singing familiar hymns and learning new hymns or choruses is a way a local church can richly participate in its fellowship. In the Zimbabwe Episcopal Area, singing competitions are held for church choirs and other church groups, promoting fellowship within the church.

(c) The need to fellowship around food: I grew up at Sherukuru United Methodist Church, where there was a fellowship practice that I often think about. As we came toward Christmas, the church people bought an ox or cow from somebody in the community. If they did not have money to pay for the beast, they would work for whoever offered such a beast. The day before Christmas the beast was slaughtered, and everybody came together for fellowship at the church. All Christian members of the local church in the community were welcome. People ate together during the day, and in the evening gathered to sing, watch a dramatic play, or listen to children recite poems. At these multigenerational gatherings, fellowship and *koinonia* was on display in the local church.

Second, often a church that recognizes its nature as a fellowship church in Christ is bound to be a caring church in the community. Jesus presented his message through parables—short, simple stories that taught moral, religious, or life-situation lessons. A local church that is going to be community-conscious and a caring church will take its biblical and theological cue from the following two parables that Jesus shared with his disciples.

(a) In the first parable, Jesus talked about a man travelling from Jerusalem to Jericho who fell into the hands of robbers. After being stripped of his clothes and beaten, the man was left almost dead. A priest and Levite who saw the helpless man on the road gave no assistance. A Samaritan who also saw him attended to the victim by applying first aid and taking the man to an inn, where he paid two silver coins—an amount that would pay for two months' stay in the inn. The Samaritan was prepared to pay for any extra financial expenses. That act of attending to a robbery victim by a man who was neither a religious leader or a Jew but a hated foreigner—viewed as half-breed Samaritan both physically and spiritually—earned the Samaritan the title "good Samaritan" and "neighbor to the man who fell into the hands of robbers" (Luke 10:25–37).

(b) In the second parable, Jesus talked about judgement that will come to all nations as they gather before him. Like a shepherd, he would separate sheep from the goats, and put sheep on his right and goats on his left. Then he will say to those on his right:

> Come, you who are blessed by my Father; take your inheritance, the kingdom prepared for you since the creation of the world. For I was hungry and you gave me something to eat, I was thirsty and you gave me something to drink, I was a stranger and you invited me in, I needed clothes and you clothed me, I was sick and you looked after me, I was in prison and you came to visit me. (Matt. 25:34–36)

The parable of the righteous ends with the following words, "I tell you, whatever you did for one of the least of these brothers and sisters of mine, you did for me" (Matt. 25:40). Every local church has a challenge to discern the various people and groups of people who have needs in its community, for among such persons, God is at work already. There are a number of things that a local church can do to join in God's work in its community.

First, search for the needy. Look for the hungry, the naked, the poor, the sick, the abandoned elderly, and other needy persons in your community. For example, we in African local churches need to consider how we have responded to the following mission issues: HIV and AIDS pandemic, violence in our communities, poverty stricken families, and many other issues. I shall comment on two issues:

(a) On HIV and AIDS, it is sad to be a worshipping congregation where the pastor or a lay preacher condemns or stigmatizes persons suffering from the pandemic as sinners who deserve punishment. The church of Christ has no other choice but to love and accept those infected by the pandemic, and to stand with the affected families. At funerals I have heard people including Christians accusing other families of witchcraft when it was clear that the deceased died of AIDS. Our local churches should champion the efforts to share true information about HIV and AIDS in order to dispel both superstition and fear, and teach people to love one another, in spite of what the pandemic has inflicted on us. As John taught, ". . . perfect love drives out fear" (1 John 4:18).

(b) There is violence everywhere—in our African villages, in the fields, in our cities—often the result of political power struggles. People are killed in daylight, and houses set on fire. Some perpetrators of such violence may be our neighbours or fellow Christians who happen to belong to another political party. Christians should not forget that in the struggle for political change we may have a lot to lose if we do not look after one another as God expects us to. Like the spies Joshua and Rahab, the prostitute of the city of Jericho, we need to look far ahead in life and make a binding oath, "Our lives for your lives!", in order to partake in the blessings of the promised land (Josh. 2:14), and the potential God has prepared for us in life.

Second, support the work of some good agencies. One day John told Jesus that he and other disciples had come across a man who was driving out demons in Jesus' name. He said that they tried to stop him because he was not part of their team. Jesus responded, "Do not stop him . . . for whoever is not against you is for you" (Luke 9:50). There are organizations in our communities that are concerned with the control of epidemics, the purification of water, improvement of home sanitation, family care, mosquito control, nutrition instruction, and many other good things. Even though their approach may be different from ours, the local church should respect these organizations, for they are not our enemies.

At times we may need to team with these organizations operating in our communities to carry out some of the services for people in the community, rather than simply hoping the church will do it alone. We may invite some of the professional people to share their insights with our committees on education for children, medical concerns, and other issues in our communities. A caring church can be salt and light for its community through joining with other groups with the same mission.

The Healing and Redemptive Church

Today, almost every African country is bombarded by a number of prophets claiming to heal the sick. Often, the healing ministry is misunderstood, and some Christians may feel uncomfortable each time the subject of healing comes up. Jesus as the Messiah is the one who brought "health and salvation."[13] Jesus perceived that connection "between his healing ministry and his redemptive ministry."[14] Hence he said, "It is not the healthy who need a doctor, but the sick. I have not come to call the righteous, but sinners" (Mark 2:17). Jesus considered himself to be the redeemer and physician for humankind. It was for that reason that the early church had an order of "healers" in the ministry of the New Testament Church (cf. "miracles, then gifts of healing" 1 Cor. 12:28; cf. 12:9, where "gifts of healings" are mentioned as among the gifts of the Spirit).[15] Also, note James 5:3–16, where it stresses the connection between forgiveness and healing, and mentions the anointing of the sick with oil in the name of the Lord. There is power to heal in every local church.

Kathy Black, Professor of Homiletics at the Claremont School of Theology, makes a distinction between two words often used interchangeably—*cure* and *healing*. She describes cure as at least eliminating the symptoms if not the disease itself, whereas healing is expressed through the use of the phrases *healing presence*, *healing moment*, and *healing service*.[16] Black points out, "Each of these images elicits a sense of peace and well-being, but they do not imply cure." She goes on to say:

> While a healing worship service may include hope and even prayer for a cure for a particular individual, the intent of the service is to bring some sense of well-being into the person's life, a sense of comfort, support, and peace. [For example] Linda is blind and will be physically blind for the rest of her life, but she can still experience much healing in the midst of her blindness.[17]

Black quotes John Kleich who said, ". . . healing entails finding some sense of meaning in the midst of one's situation, some sense of well-being in spite of the illness . . . healing of illness takes place always, infallibly, since everyone ultimately finds some meaning to the life situations."[18] Black herself has a disability, but she made her position clear, "I am first and foremost a person; hence I am a '*person* with a disability.'"[19]

The distinction that Black makes between the words *cure* and *healing* is important. This is one of the reasons some Christians in our local churches move from one church to another. They often seek not healing but cure. When they see what is presented on television, which demonstrates cure, or hear of some charismatic churches that proclaim primarily cure, they become attracted to such proclamation. There is need in our local churches to show people that Christian proclamation on healing is holistic; it is both healing and redemptive to the total person. Christian understanding of healing is that it brings healing into all our relations, with one's self, with neighbours, and with God. So we can plan for *healing services* in our local churches. As Kathy Black said above, "The intent of the service is to bring some sense of well-being into the person's life, a sense of comfort, support, and peace."

In 1961, the Reverend Larry Eisenberg, a missionary who recently had come to Rhodesia from the United States, was appointed pastor at Ehnes Memorial Church, Old Mutare Mission. Prior to coming to Rhodesia, Larry had had some experiences with the General Board of Discipleship of The United Methodist Church in Nashville, Tennessee, USA. I was also appointed an associate pastor to the same congregation from January until July 1961, when I left for my studies in the United States. Sometime in February of the same year, Larry and I talked with the leadership of Ehnes Memorial Church about holding a healing worship service on the first Thursday of the month, for one to one-and-a-half hours. The leadership of the congregation fully welcomed the idea. At the outset, the pastor made it clear that expectations should not be focused on dramatic cases of cure from illnesses and diseases, although that was not ruled out. Rather, the intent of the healing service was healing as individuals and as a congregation. This kind of exhortation enabled people to become conscious of God's presence in our midst, and enabled them to present themselves to him in whatever manner the Spirit directed them.

For the few months I was present before leaving for school and the ensuing period after I had gone, the results were as follows. (a) There were no dramatic cases of persons who were cured. (b) Several members of Ehnes Memorial Church remarked on a new spiritual awareness of God's presence in their lives, and an improvement in the general well-being of relations between missionaries and the nationals, the authorities of the mission centre and students, and also the general labourers. Some members of the church who previously had felt they were not good enough to be members of Ehnes Memorial Church felt a newness of spirit of fellowship. (c) The special Thursday evening service drew a number of people who came from outside the Old Mutare Mission area.

I have always viewed that experience as a benchmark of my understanding of the ministry of healing. Healing in the name of Christ may include cure, while in other cases we may have to learn from Paul's experience when the Lord said to him, "My grace is sufficient for you, for my power is made perfect in weakness" (2 Cor. 12:9). Both cure and healing are God's prerogative, and we must constantly expect anything to happen as we present ourselves and others in prayer to him.

There are a number of ways to promote the belief and practice of the ministry of healing, and it does not have to be carried out uniformly as such. Every local church will have to find ways that suit its particular situation. The common denominator that all local churches share is that each church is surrounded by persons who need healing of one sort or another. The following are ways that some local churches have used to promote this ministry of healing.

First, an invitation to healing before the pastoral prayer or preaching: Some pastors invite people who have burdens and are weary or are sick to come to the kneeling rail of the altar before the pastoral prayer. Others pray in response to special requests from members of the congregation just before the pastor preaches. Whichever way one chooses, the idea is to recognize persons who may be hurting—the bereaved, those with loved ones seriously ill, those struggling with issues of justice in society, the hungry, the homeless, and many others. This invitation is recognition of Christ's presence among his people. He is the Christ who is ready to unburden the burdened, gives support and acceptance to all, and opens those healed to the worship of God in spirit and in truth. This is what we talked about above as "healing presence"—the Lord's presence among his people.

Second, specific invitation for those seeking healing or even cure: The pastor may extend an invitation to members in need of healing to remain behind after the service. Such persons are often instructed to kneel at the altar rail, where the pastor and other leaders of the church will pray for them. It is important for the pastor to ask each person individually what concerns or problems he or she has. Giving the individual who is seeking healing an opportunity to unburden his/her concern is a necessary part of the healing process. It is also absolutely important for the person seeking healing to be open and honest with the pastor about the problem, including all that the individual has tried to do about the problem. At this point, the individual seeking healing and those praying need to focus their faith in Christ Jesus, the physician of human beings. By submitting themselves to God body and spirit they enter in power, and at the same time evoke the Holy Spirit to help in their weakness, for there are times or situations when we do not know what to say, and yet the Spirit will intercede for us (Rom. 8:26).

We should not fear failure in this ministry of healing, for it is God alone who heals his people, and not us. Ours is to believe as Christ taught his disciples, "Whatever you ask for in prayer, believe that you have received it, and it will be yours" (Mark 11:24). When God has blessed your ministry with positive results, it is not something to brag or boast about. Rather, like Peter and John we could also say it is the God of our ancestors, "the God of our fathers [who] has glorified his servant Jesus" (Acts 3:13). The pastor does not take pride in his own powers or reputation. Rather, he may want to learn from the ancient priest of Israel, Eli, who said to Hannah concerning her childlessness, "Go in peace, and may the God of Israel grant you what you have asked of him" (1 Sam. 1:17).

Third, an appeal for healing of the sick: Mainline churches face a concern that people leave their local churches to join a new charismatic one that claims to have power to heal the sick. This is likely because in many mainline churches healing has been avoided altogether, while in the charismatic churches healing is regarded purely as "cure." Television programmes that feature charismatic pastors may influence the sick to go to their churches or even to fly to neighbouring countries seeking healing.

How can a local church demonstrate that it is an agent of God's healing and redemptive power to individuals and to communities today? Jesus had a fabulous ministry for the sick that injected new faith and hope in them. He healed Simon's mother-in-law who suffered from a fever (Mark 1:20f), he healed a man with leprosy (Mark 1:41), and many others. Similarly, this power was witnessed in the life of the early church with Peter and John healing a crippled beggar (Acts 3:6ff), with Paul shaking off a snake into the fire without suffering any ill effects on the Shore of Malta (Acts 28:1ff), and many other incidents.

A more relevant incident occurred in a revival that broke out in the Zimbabwe Episcopal area in June or July 1918. God used three pastor-teachers, John Cheke, David Mandisodza, and Gezana Sadomba to instantaneously heal Nhenhu, a daughter of the Chieftess Muredzwa of Zinyembe. At the age of six years, Nhenhu's hands and legs became deformed, so that she spent all her time lying down and had to be carried everywhere. In spite of consultations with traditional healers, nothing helped her. In 1918, as the revival spread in Chief Mutasa's area, about thirty kilometres northeast of Old Mutare Mission, Nhenhu, who was now a young woman, heard about the three pastor-teachers who were visiting and preaching in the area. Nhenhu shared with her mother the Chieftess her desire to invite the preachers to her home to pray for her.

The three pastor-teachers gladly went to the Chieftess's home, accompanied by other Christians. After songs and prayer, Gezana held Nhenhu from her armpits, with Mandisodza laying his hands on her head. While everybody was in the spirit of prayer and great expectation,

John Cheke repeated the Apostle's words: "In the name of Jesus Christ of Nazareth, walk" (Acts 3:6). As they lifted her, for the first time in a long time, Nhenhu stood and walked. Thereafter, Nhenhu is said to have lived a normal life, and was a member of the United Methodist Church until her death in 1972.[20]

People in our communities are hurting—the sick, the bereaved, families with conflicts, those who have lost property due to political upheaval and natural disasters, those who have not found justice for their grievances, These persons are searching for pastors and local congregations that can provide them with healing and redemption from all these evils. And they are searching for genuine Christian healing that will transform their total being—physical body, spirit, and social dimensions of their lives. Some pastors are already doing wonderful healing ministry in their churches, and we pray for more pastors and more mainline local churches to open their doors for the ministry of healing for the sick.

The Church and the Contextualization of the Faith

The church of Christ in mission must learn to theologize for itself, and to contextualize the faith in its own setting. Conversion to the Christian faith should not mean that new converts are subjugated to the cultural practices of the one who brings the new faith to a people. Rather, it should be that cultural and religious expectations and dreams are fulfilled in their contextual situation or setting. Two issues of immediate concern to the African church are: (a) the large number of probationary members due to their marriage status, and (b) the relationship of the Christian faith and the *n'anga* institution in Africa.

First, we'll look at the large number of probationary members in church due to their marriage status. In Zimbabwe there are three types of marriage rites: (a) Civil marriage, conducted by the magistrate, which is exclusively monogamous (and often mistakenly called the Christian marriage). To others, this type of marriage may simply be European or western. Pastors can be registered to conduct such marriages on behalf of the state. (b) Customary law marriage, also conducted by the magistrate, which allows polygamy. (c) Customary law marriage since 1997, which although not registered is recognized by government. Like the other two types of marriage, it authorizes inheritance of property, including support for children in the event of separation or divorce. Many people in Zimbabwe continue to marry under the customary law, a marriage not recognized by some of the mainline churches.

The customary law marriage has its weaknesses, but it remains a valid option to many people in Africa. Its conditions at times may be violated, but in the long run are fulfilled. By and large, the customary law marriage is the only type of marriage that our great-grandparents and grandparents knew, and it is still acceptable to civil society. In Zimbabwe, anybody who marries begins with a customary law marriage. That means in reality some Africans in Zimbabwe end up married under two types of marriages: first under the customary law marriage, and second either under civil marriage or registered customary law marriage.

Unfortunately, many of the mainline churches in Africa only accept the exclusively monogamous civil marriage conducted by the magistrate and pastors registered to conduct such marriages on behalf of the state. This type of marriage alone has been deemed Christian. But most persons married under customary law marriage in many regions of Africa today have only one wife.

In the United Methodist Church in Zimbabwe, if a couple married under a customary law marriage is converted and decides to join the church, they have to be married again under the civil marriage if they are to gain full membership. Some probationary members who have not married under the civil marriage end up as permanent probationary members, or backsliders, or join other churches where they are afforded full church membership.

When both colonial governments and the churches came to Africa, Africans were practicing the customary law marriage. There came a time when both colonialists and missionaries set out to obliterate all that was African in favour of western ways, including marriage practices. So the western civil marriage, conducted by the magistrate and registered clergy, and which was exclusively monogamous, was considered by mainline churches or "missionary churches" as Christian marriage. But that type of marriage in reality is more European or western than Christian. Some people have rightly labelled it a "white wedding," which has frightened away some who would otherwise become strong followers of Christ.

Are churches that reject the customary law marriage burdening seeking disciples with a yoke that is unnecessarily heavy for them (Acts 15:10)? Do Africans really need to be under two types of marriages to be Christian? As Africans and especially as African Christians we may need to find a way to Christianize the customary law marriage and accept it as a blessing to God's people, beginning with those who already enjoy a monogamous customary law marriage.

Second, we will examine evangelisation and African traditional healing ways. On 11 October 2006, BBC presented a programme concerning the menace of malaria in Ghana. The narrator of the programme shared that malaria was still a great killer worldwide, especially in Africa. Children were said to be more susceptible to malaria than adults. Interestingly, in Ghana they found that people suffering from malaria responded more favourably to a treatment of Chinese traditional medicine than other more "modern" treatments. Increasingly, we see Chinese and Indian traditional medicines, especially herbs, being used in African countries. At the same time, consumers of such foreign traditional medicines condemn African traditional herbs and roots as the work of the devil.

Some African governments through their Ministries of Health have come up with ways to accept and co-opt the practice of African traditional medicine as well as the acceptable traditional skills of the *n'anga* (traditional healer) in treating patients. Lately we have witnessed a number of both local and foreign researchers in our countries who have made advances in the studies of African medicinal herbs and roots, some of which we understand are already used to make drugs. These researchers are guided by some of our *n'anga* or traditional herbalists in this study. Do churches in Africa wait to be taught by foreigners the value and importance of Africa's medicinal herbs? Or do the churches wait for their governments to take the lead in sharing the "gospel" of African herbal medicine first while they continue condemning it as the work of the devil?

In spite of all the resounding sermons that are preached condemning African medicine and the *n'anga*, many of our church members still consult both. Essentially, the church is attacking innocent institutions of Africa that could be a blessing to many. At times, we criticize to show how "civilised" we are according to the national consciousness of other people, rather than how "evangelised." Often, by our condemnation we force Christians to go to the *n'anga* at night for fear of being seen by others. We make them hypocrites.

Jesus challenged the leaders of his time when he said: "Woe to you, teachers of the law and Pharisees, you hypocrites! You travel over land and sea to win a single convert, and when you have succeeded, you make them twice as much a child of hell as you are" (Matt. 23:13–15). And, according to Luke, Jesus gave a stern warning to those who cause others "to sin" (Luke 17:2).

For many people, especially those who live in rural areas, hospitals and clinics are far away and too expensive to afford. Where can the people go, especially when churches themselves do not seem to believe in healing ministry as taught by James 5:13ff?

John Wesley would have sympathised with the African Christians who opt to use African traditional herbs and roots. Wesley lived in the eighteenth century when the only three medical schools of the United Kingdom—Oxford, Cambridge, and Edinburgh—all together graduated only about twenty-four medical doctors a year.[21] With a population ranging between five and nine million, there was a scarcity of medical doctors. Additionally, the poor could not afford the fees that these physicians charged for their services.[22] Wesley was concerned for the welfare of the poor, not only for the "physic or the art of healing."[23] Wesley's book *Primitive Physic* was his effort to search for remedies or other options so that the poor could have access to healing—healing he assigned "a divine original."[24]

While Wesley used the word *primitive*, we African Christians use *traditional*. Wesley has already told us that the word *physic* means the art of healing. Thus we could easily translate the title of his book *Primitive Physic* to mean "Traditional Art of Healing." Listen to Wesley himself:

> Thus far physic was wholly found on experiment. The European, as well as the American, said to his neighbour, "Are you sick? Drink the juice of this herb, and your sickness will be at an end. Are you in a burning heat? Leap into the river, and then sweat till you are well. Has the snake bitten you? Chew and apply that root, and the poison will not hurt you." The ancient men, having a little experience joined with common sense, and common humanity, cured both themselves and their neighbours of most of the distempers to which every nation was subjected.[25]

The institution of African traditional healing is not perfect. However, we need to avoid sweeping judgements that it is all the work of darkness or the work of the devil. John Wesley would have had no problem with African traditional healing; instead he would have searched for as many herbs and roots as he could find to help cure the sick. He would also talk to many *n'anga* in an effort to understand their skills and knowledge, and those grey areas of their art of which we tend to be suspicious. He would do this for the sake of offering helpful and constructive education to Christians and all the people concerned.

We need not condemn the whole institution of African traditional healing because of a few people who abuse their knowledge. On one hand, I can understand and forgive the missionaries who first condemned African traditional healing; but I find it difficult to understand a church in Africa with all African leadership still condemning what I would consider African genius.

I have had the opportunity to conduct several workshops called "Two by Two Lay Visitation Evangelism Programme." One of the advantages of this approach to evangelism is that it brings the local church and the pastor face-to-face with people in their homes. It may bring the local church members in contact with people who are hurting in ways they might not have known. We may meet people such as Hannah, a childless mother (1 Sam. 1:2ff), or the man with leprosy who managed to come to Jesus and knelt before him, saying, "Lord, if you are willing, you can make me clean" (Matt. 8:2). Indeed, in our communities we meet people who are hurting and always wondering with whom to share their burdens.

The two-by-two lay visitation evangelism programme commissions the local church to go into its community and offer Christ to people through listening and talking to them. It is not easy to offer Christ unless one understands why one needs Christ. We train members of the local church to do the following in their visitation: (a) Determine whether their visit is an *evangelistic visit* (meaning someone who does not confess Christ as his Saviour and Lord), or a *friendly visit* (to a backslider), or a *shut-in visit* (an elderly, disabled, or sick person). (b) Give the person visited the opportunity to share with the two visitors any concerns that he or she has. And, (c) Offer the members of the local church the opportunity to minister or bring a healing ministry to such persons through word or deed.

Bishop Abel Tendekayi Muzorewa recently published a book entitled *Evangelism that Decolonizes the Soul*. The title of this book is packed with truth regarding the church in Africa. Evangelisation is meant to decolonize our soul, and liberate our mind so that we begin to evolve a new identity around Christ as African Christians. That means there is need to make an intentional move toward having Christians whose faith in Christ and the African culture find reconciliation in God (2 Cor. 5:19), and an African Christianity that is tempered by the gospel of Jesus Christ and yet coloured by the African cultures. African Christians need to move confidently in attaining the kind of liberating Christianity to which John testifies, "The glory of God gives it light, and the Lamb is its lamp. The nations will walk by its light, and the kings of the earth will bring their splendor into it" (Rev. 21:23–24).

Chapter 12

Historical Development of the Ministry

With the rapid development and expansion of the early church throughout the Roman Empire in the first and second centuries, two different types of leadership evolved within the church—the charismatic and the congregational or institutional leadership. The charismatic leadership included apostles, prophets, evangelists, and teachers. The congregational or institutional leadership included apostles, elders, and deacons. While the charismatic leadership served to show the unity of the church of Christ, the congregational leadership showed the locality of the church as it was planted among the peoples of all nations.

The Rise of Church Offices for Ministry

If the preaching of Peter on the day of Pentecost marked a new order of charismatic proclamation (Acts 2:14–41), equally important was the appointment of the seven deacons by the apostles (Acts 6:1–7), which was a clear signal of what was coming—the need for ministries of caring, orderliness, and the administration of the church.

First, the office of apostles is the office of the church, but it was not created by the church. Rather, it was created by Jesus Christ himself, for those whom he chose and designated apostles, and he commissioned them to take the gospel to all nations on earth (Mark 16:15, Matt. 28:19–20). The word *apostolos* simply means "envoy," "accredited representative,"[1] or "one sent forth."[2] Even Paul understood his apostleship in the same manner, as he related his calling to the churches in Galatia: "But when God, who set me apart from birth and called me by his grace, was pleased to reveal his Son in me so that I might preach him among the Gentiles . . ." (Gal. 1:15–16).

In the New Testament, the word *apostle* is also used in a broader sense. For example, it is used of Barnabas as well as of Paul (Acts 14:4, 14), of Andronicus, and Junias (Rom. 16:7). Two unnamed brethren are called "apostles of the churches," Epaphroditus is referred to as "your apostle" (Phil. 2:25), and it is used of Paul, Silas, and Timothy (1 Thess. 2:6).[3] However, it remains that the word *apostle* in its regular use:

> . . . means "an apostle of Jesus Christ" (in the opening words of 1 Cor., 2 Cor., Eph., Col., and 1 Tim., 2 Tim., Titus); "an apostle, not by human appointment or human commission, but by commission from the Lord Jesus Christ and from God the Father who raised him from the dead" (Gal. 1:1); and so, in the latter part of 2 Corinthians, he speaks in 10:8 of an "authority given by the Lord to build you up, not pull you down," and the same phrase, word for word the same in the Greek, in 13:10, right at the end.[4]

The apostles had both the mandate and the charisma from the Lord to establish his church in all the nations. Because of that unique apostolic authority, from Luke's account in Acts it is clear that the twelve apostles, including Paul, were received as the leaders of the church of Christ, whether in Palestine or in the Gentile world. The main responsibility of the apostles was preaching Christ (Acts 6:2, 4) and founding congregations (Acts 13–19). Again, apostleship was not an office of the church, for it originated with Christ himself. In so far as the leadership of the congregation in Jerusalem was concerned:

> The dominant authority was at first Peter, as is testified by Mt. 16:17–19, Lk. 22:31f, and by the role that Peter played both in the synoptic traditions as a whole and in

> Paul. Besides him, John, the son of Zebedee, and James, the Lord's brother, must soon have won a leading position; Paul speaks of those three as the "pillars" (Gal. 2:9, cf. 1:18f).[5]

Then when Peter and John had left Jerusalem, the Lord's brother James remained the recognised authority (Acts 12:17, 21:18). He had become chairman of the elders of the Jerusalem church.

Second, we'll look at the office of prophets. By 46 and 48 CE, when Paul's first missionary journey took place, the church in Antioch already had prophets and teachers (Acts 13:1). In writing to the church at Corinth from Ephesus "in the early months of CE 54 or possibly towards the end of 53,"[6] Paul, who could have been at the end of his second missionary journey,[7] wrote about some of the church offices that were already in operation: "And God has placed in the church first of all apostles, second prophets, third teachers . . ." (1 Cor. 12:28). In his letter to the saints in Ephesus (if it was Paul who wrote it) which is dated just before 95 CE,[8] (suggesting that the letter may have been written after Paul), he says, "So Christ himself gave the apostles, the prophets, the evangelists, the pastors and teachers, to equip his people for works of service" (Eph. 4:11–12). According to the two letters mentioned above, the office of prophecy comes second to that of the apostles in both lists. Prophecy in the early church was not different from prophecy in the Old Testament. "For prophecy was but the greatest of those spiritual *charismata*—speaking with tongues, seeing visions, receiving revelations, etc.,—with which it was closely allied and of which it is the type."[9] It found its utterances in "exhortation, instruction, encouragement, and consolation—aids which are now conveyed by means of preaching."[10] Its focus was proclamation of Christ and teaching. "The true spirit of prophecy was evidenced in bearing witness to Jesus."[11] The gift of prophecy was not confined to one gender. So we learn of Philip's daughters who prophesied (Acts 21:9).

"The leading prophets of the first era soon won a pre-eminent position in the Christian tradition"[12] as they became closely associated with the apostles in proclaiming the gospel. As such, the office of prophecy belonged to the *charismatic* leadership of the church. However, the position of prophets in the church was not considered as an office. The prophets were called for the whole church. According to Barclay, "Their message was held to be not the result of thought and study but direct result of the Holy Spirit. They had no homes and no families and no means of support. They went from church to church proclaiming the will of God as God had told it to them."[13]

The office of prophecy in the first century was so close to that of the apostles that Paul in writing to the Ephesians said, "Consequently, you are no longer foreigners and strangers, but fellow citizens with God's people and also members of his household, built on the foundation of the apostles and prophets, with Christ Jesus himself as the chief cornerstone" (Eph. 2:19–20). In his letter to the church at Corinth, Paul writes, "For no one can lay any foundation other than the one already laid, which is Jesus Christ" (1 Cor. 3:11). Again, in the letter to the church at Ephesus, Paul (if it is Paul) is "ranking himself with his fellow apostles as the foundation itself."[14] However, Francis Beare is right in pointing out:

> The prophets, of course, are the Christian prophets (cf.4:ii; 1 Cor. 14:1–5, 24ff; Acts 11:27ff). This bracketing of prophets with apostles has no real parallel in the genuine epistles. It might be observed that as early as Polycarp [Bishop of Smyrna 110–56], the office of prophet in the church has fallen so completely into desuetude [disuse] that the martyr bishop can use the word only of the O.T. prophets, "The apostles who preached the gospel to us, and the prophets who proclaimed in advance the coming of the Lord."[15]

Richard Rackham points out that there arose another class of less eminent prophets who regarded prophecy as a profession, and places Agabus in this category (Acts 11:28, 21:10). Apparently, it was partly due to this group of prophets that prophecy deteriorated and lost its reputation in the early church. Barclay echoes those sentiments when he writes:

> The prophets became a problem . . . The office of prophet was singularly liable to abuse. These prophetic wanderers had considerable prestige. Some of them abused their office and made it an excuse for living a very comfortable life at the expense of the congregations whom they visited.[16]

No wonder the apostles exhorted the early church on how to handle prophecy. Paul writes to the church of the Thessalonians, "Do not quench the Spirit. Do not treat prophecies with contempt but test them all" (1 Thess. 5:19–21). John writes, "Dear friends, do not believe every spirit, but test the spirits to see whether they are from God, because many false prophets have gone out into the world" (1 John 4:1).

What a lesson to our the present generation of Christians, especially in Africa where so many preachers are emerging claiming to be prophets and live very comfortable lives at the expense of the poor who are desperate, oppressed, and harassed day in and day out.

Third, there is the office of teachers. Like the prophets, teachers also belonged to the *charismatic* leadership of the church. During the initial period of the early church, teachers ranked third among the offices of the church (1 Cor. 12:28), and later, close to the end of the first century and early in the second century, they ranked fourth, together with pastors (Eph. 4:11). The apostles were the best and only authorised teachers when it came to imparting knowledge of Christ, for they had witnessed everything about him from the beginning (1 John 1:1f). It was for that reason that the early church in Jerusalem "devoted themselves to the apostles' teaching" (Acts 2:42). It happened that those who were prophets were also teachers. In Antioch, we are not so sure who were prophets and who were teachers (Acts 13:1f). One assumes that the five exercised their gifts as prophets as well as teachers (Acts 11:26, 15:35).

As the numbers of disciples increased each day with the expansion of the geographical areas reached by the gospel, a class of teachers emerged in the early church. The necessity of preserving the right teaching had arisen, as that is mentioned again and again in the pastoral letters (1 Tim. 4:11, Titus 2:1f). It was for this reason that the apostles wrote to the churches so that they would learn the sound doctrine of the Christian faith. It was also for the same reason that great teachers like Pantaenus established a catechetical school for believers in Alexandria.[17] According to Eusebius, Pantaenus travelled to the East, as far as India, to preach the gospel of Christ.[18] Similarly, in the second century, Pamphilus, another great teacher who was dedicated to the spread of sound learning, established a school of theology at Caesarea.[19]

The substance of their teaching was Jesus Christ and sound doctrine of the faith. The incumbents were as dependent on the guidance of the Holy Spirit as the prophets (1 Cor. 12:28, Acts 13:1). They were also wanderers from one church to another like the prophets. The earlier teachers could have been more akin to what we know as catechists, and later they were like philosophers.[20] Clement of Alexandria and Origen, his successor at the catechetical school in about 203 CE, were teachers who were also philosophers. Origen is regarded as "the most brilliant and original thinker the church had yet seen,"[21] and could have been one of the last universal great teachers of the early church. The office of teachers is said to have remained prominent much longer in the life of the church than the offices of prophets and evangelists.[22]

Fourth is the office of evangelists. We have already noted that although the office of the evangelists is not mentioned in Paul's list in his letter to all called to be saints in Rome (Rom. 12:28), in the letter to the Ephesians the office is ranked third. The task of the evangelist was to proclaim Christ to men and women, Jews and Gentiles, without any discrimination. That is the task Philip and some of the Jewish disciples who fled the persecution that erupted in Jerusalem following the stoning of Stephen were doing in Samaria (Acts 8:4ff). Those men or evangelists "from Cyprus and Cyrene, went to Antioch and began to speak to the Greeks also, telling them the good news about the Lord Jesus" (Acts 11:20). The evangelists were what we would consider missionaries today. The evangelists were part of the *charismatic* leadership of the church, which included not only the apostles themselves but the prophets and teachers who wandered from place to place proclaiming Christ, and founding churches. It is reported that "in the earliest times, no doubt, the activity of the apostles was not rigidly distinguished from that of evangelists."[23] For example, Eusebius who wrote probably in the fourth century says:

> At once, in accordance with the Holy Scriptures, the voice of its inspired evangelists and the apostles went forth into all the earth, and their words to the ends of the world [Ps. 19:4]. In every town and village, like a well-filled threshing-floor, churches shot up bursting with eager members.[24]

There are only three references that specifically speak about evangelists in the Bible: Acts 21:8, Ephesians 4:11, and 2 Timothy 4:5. Nevertheless, there were many evangelists in the early church. A preacher such as Epaphras, who brought the good news of Jesus Christ to Colossae, was an evangelist. Priscilla and Aquila, who invited Apollos to their home and shared with him "the way of God more adequately" (Acts 18:26ff), were evangelists. In the third century, the authors of the canonical gospels were referred to as evangelists, as in their writings they were bearers of the good news of Jesus Christ[25] into the whole world.

Again, the charismatic leadership served to demonstrate the unity of the church of Christ—those leaders were warmly welcomed wherever they went as they faithfully proclaimed and taught the gospel of Jesus Christ. To reiterate, the charismatic leadership of the church included apostles, prophets, teachers, and evangelists, who were all wandering preachers, planting churches in various nations of the Roman Empire on the foundational message of Jesus Christ, the Son of God and Saviour of the world.

Fifth, we find the office of elders. Earlier on, we saw that the appointment of the deacons by the apostles was a sign of what was yet to come. As much as the church was catholic or universal, it had to be localized and so did its leadership. Thus, the local congregation had to be planted in a geographical, cultural, and socio-economic environment where it reflected the identity of its locality. Following the appointment of deacons by the apostles, who served in congregations, another important church leadership position that was established by the apostles was that of the elders. The authority of the apostles to plant churches and to appoint the congregational leadership made the apostles not only charismatic leaders, but also congregational or institutional leaders of the church of Christ. Hence, the congregations they founded became known as apostolic congregations, which in time played a significant role in defining the rule of faith and the canonization of the Christian scriptures. The tradition of elders is a Jewish principle of authority that was found in every village, town, and city. It is well represented in the time of Moses, when he appointed seventy elders of Israel, and went up the mountain to receive "the tablets of stone, with the law and commandments" (Exod. 24:12).

During New Testament times, that Jewish system was still functioning with the *Sanhedrin* or *Presbytery* as the chief seat of authority for the whole Jewish nation.[26] Consequently, one found the elders managing the affairs of the social and religious life of Jewish communities, including in their synagogues. It is not surprising that as soon as the Palestinian congregations were formed, "the office of the *elders* appeared."[27] That practice followed the Jewish synagogue pattern. It is interesting to note that when the church at Antioch made its contribution for famine relief to the mother-church in Jerusalem by Barnabas and Paul in about 46 CE, that gift was handed over to the elders (Acts 11:30), not to the apostles.[28] "The elders of the Jerusalem church, among whom James the brother of Jesus was *primus inter pares*, seem to have constituted a kind of Nazarene Sanhedrin, distinct from the twelve apostles."[29]

The introduction of elders into the administration of the church came with it the ritual of ordination in the Christian church. The verb "to ordain" means "to decree or to order or establish or invest with functions or office of a minister, priest or rabbi."[30] Therefore, ordination means being ordained. In the Old Testament, the Psalmist acknowledges that God established or ordained (KJV) the government of the universe, when he said, "When I consider your heavens, the work of your fingers, the moon and the stars, which you have set in place, what is mankind that you are mindful of them, human beings that you care for them?" (Ps. 8:3–4).

The wonder that the Psalmist expresses is the wonder we experience every day in nature. For example, each time we see fire, we believe it burns; and it does burn. If we see ice, we know it is cold; and it is cold. These are principles that are established in our natural environment or context. We have learned that when a woman conceives a child today, in about nine months a baby will be born. Such are the principles that have been ordained in nature; and as believers we acknowledge that these are principles ordained in God's creation.

In the history of the Old Testament we see that God ordained certain persons with authority and to delegate such authority to others.[31] Moses is ordered by the Lord to delegate authority to Joshua by means of laying hands (Num. 27:18–23). Similarly, Jeremiah is ordained while still in the womb of his mother (Jer. 1:5). The idea of ordination to a function becomes more pronounced in the New Testament. For example, Jesus appointed and designated or ordained the twelve apostles—that "they might be with him and that he might send them out to preach and to have authority to drive out demons" (Mark 3:14–15). The seven deacons were ordained for a special responsibility of daily distribution of food to the Hebraic and Grecian widows in Jerusalem (Acts 6:5–6). Paul was ordained and appointed an apostle to the Gentiles (Gal. 1:15), and Paul and Barnabas began appointing and ordaining elders for the churches they founded (Acts 14:23).

According to Bultmann, the *charismatics*, so far as they were proclaimers of the word, "more and more became officials; that is their *charisma*, which was originally given to a person, is now understood as an *office-charisma* conveyed by ordination (1 Tim. 4:14, 2 Tim. 1:6)."[32] That is, some of the wandering evangelists settled down as appointees of the apostles in local communities. No wonder that later on we see Timothy at Ephesus and Titus at Crete.

Initially in the early church the title *presbyteroi* (elders) denoted both age and office (1 Pet. 5:1–5).[33] In Gentile congregations, a leader or an elder was called *episkopos*, which in the Greek usage "was the title of certain municipal officials and also of officers of associations and cultic societies."[34] Christian *episkopoi* appear for the first time in Philippians 1:1 and there *diakonoi* are named with them.[35] That means the office of *elders* in the Jewish congregations and *episkopoi* in the Gentile congregations were the same. "The difference between *presbyters* and *episkopoi* is probably just a difference of terminology."[36] Thus, the terms *presbyteroi* and *eposkpoi* both meant *elders*—the leaders of the congregations. The fact that the apostles founded congregations that were known as apostolic congregations and appointed elders in those congregations shows the apostles were not only charismatic leaders but also congregational leaders.

The Rise of the *Monepiskopate* or Monarchical Bishop

The distinction between the two titles, *presbyteroi* and *episkopoi* or elders and bishops, came with the development of *the monepiskopate*, meaning one bishop to one congregation. It is natural that the presbyters or elders had to have the chairmanship of the board of elders. It was with that development of selecting one elder as chairman of the presbytery that the title *episkopos* (bishop) was used exclusively to refer to the chairman of the board, while the rest retained the title *presbyteroi* (presbyters or elders).[37]

Originally, the elders were the local officials of the congregations, and their main function was to attend to the administration of their members locally. If the elders preached at all, it was not by virtue of their office. Rather, their main function was to organize their local congregations for worship and to provide hospitality to the wandering *charismatic* leaders—the apostles, prophets, evangelists, and teachers. Those elders were appointed either by the apostles from the congregations that the apostles themselves had founded or by those who had associated with the ministry of the apostles. In the course of time, changes began to take place, and the following were the factors that underpinned the changes.

(a) The apostolate gradually died out. James, the son of Zebedee, was the first of the apostles to meet a martyr's death (Acts 12:2). The rest of the apostles also are believed to have met their death by martyrdom. John, alone, following Emperor Domitian's death, returned from exile and settled at Ephesus in a congregation that had been founded by Paul. He taught the truth to them and remained there until he met his natural death during the time of Trajan (98–117).[38] John is considered to have been the last of the apostles of Jesus to die. Although no one could succeed the apostles as apostles, someone had to take over the leadership of the church of Christ on earth.

(b) In the eyes of the congregational leadership, it was noted from earlier on that the wandering prophets, teachers, and evangelists gradually became suspect.[39]

(c) There was a danger of "heresy," due to the existence of *Docetism*, especially in Asia Minor and *Gnosticism* in Alexandria, which had become acute.[40]

(d) As the church at Corinth increased in numbers and met regularly for the Lord's Supper (1 Cor. 11:17ff), there was need for orderly worship. Hence, Paul gave advice or direction in this matter of worship: "But everything should be done in a fitting and orderly way" (1 Cor. 14:40).

(e) Partly due to Paul's similar observation of disorderliness at the church of Corinth, we see leaders such as Ignatius resolving that the bishop was the designated leader of the sacramental ceremony. In his letter to the Magnesians, Ignatius wrote,

"Let the bishop preside in God's place, and the presbyters take the place of apostolic council, and let the deacons (my special favourites) be entrusted with the ministry of Jesus Christ who was with the Father from eternity and appeared at the end (of the world)."[41]

(f) Increasingly, the *charismatics*, who wandered and proclaimed the Word all over the place became officials, that is, their *charisma* that was originally given to the person is now understood as an *office-charisma* conveyed by ordination (1 Tim. 4:14, 2 Tim. 1:6). It is important to note that although the pastoral letters mark a later development to that of Paul, they "are not inconsistent with Paul's teaching."[42] Thus, with reference to Timothy, it simply means that Timothy having been selected for ordination (cf. Acts 13:1ff) under the guidance of prophecy (1 Tim. 1:18), and the laying of hands by the body of elders should be understood as "being an accompanying act—not a means,"[43] of receiving the gift. The point being made here is that the *charisma*, which was claimed to be given to the person by the Spirit, can be witnessed by the laying on of hands by the elders. This was a significant development.

(g) The proclamation of the Word is transferred as a right of duty of the office to the officials (elders or *episkopoi*) of the congregation.[44] What was even more important is "the fact that the proclamation of the Word became the affair of the congregational officials,"[45] who virtually became the leaders of the church. According to Eusebius, James, known as the Lord's brother, by virtue of his position as chairman of the board of elders of the congregation of Jerusalem, became the first bishop of that congregation.[46] It is explicitly said that the bishops and deacons perform the service of the prophets and teachers and are to be honoured as the *charismatics* (Did.15:1f).

Looking back at what was happening in the life of the early church and the various leadership groups that had evolved within the church during the first and second centuries, the rise of *monepiskopate* was inevitable. Indeed, the congregational or institutional leadership of the church had been placed in a more strategic position to take over the leadership of the church from the apostles than that of the *charismatics*—the wanderers. Irenaeus wrote and emphasized the truth regarding church tradition of the apostles that was observed in the whole world. He pointed out that he could enumerate those bishops who had been appointed in the churches by the apostles and their successors up to his time (130–200 CE).[47] Thus, for Irenaeus, the authority of the church officers comes from a chain of teaching chairs, as it was from a succession of ordinations for Augustine.[48] The elders, some of whom subsequently became bishops of their congregations, were naturally in a better position to understand the apostles and the local churches that they had founded. And above all, the leading concern in the church was "to conserve the apostolic witness, and, while showing its relevance to pagan modes of thought, to guard against the extremes of Gnostic speculation and prophetic enthusiasm."[49] That is what made the early church believe: "The bishop is the successor of the apostles, representing the localizing of the prophetic, teaching, and liturgical functions of the original apostolate. He becomes the centre of the Church's life, the living witness and guardian of its faith."[50]

Hence, the rise of the single bishop, who with his council of presbyters ruled the congregation, was built upon a closely-knit organization that would withstand the persecutions of the third century.[51] By the beginning of the second century, apart from the later organization of the dioceses, "a bishop was the bishop of a local congregation, not of a far-flung diocese."[52] The development to *monepiskopate* or monarchical bishop was orderly, and was widespread by the time of Ignatius, the Bishop of Antioch (115 CE), who in his letter to the Ephesian church was already making reference to "the bishop and presbytery."[53] That means the adaptation of a *monepiskopate* or monarchical bishop was a widespread practice in the church. For Ignatius the monarchical bishop leads worship and administers the sacrament of the Lord's Supper, becomes the priest, "whose office gives him a quality which separates him from the rest of the congregation, *making them laymen*."[54] Hence, the demand to appoint "elders" or "bishops" with qualities pertaining, not only to administration (such as "sensible," "hospitable," "no lover of money," etc., 1 Tim. 3:2ff, Tit. 1:6ff), but also teachers ("an apt teacher," 1 Tim. 3:2, 2 Tim. 2:24, Tit. 1:9) who are "able to give instruction in sound doctrine and also to confute those who contradict it (cf. 2 Tim. 2:24–26)."[55]

Thus, *bishop* came to mean the bishop of a local congregation, who also had a presbytery—a council of elders that worked closely with the bishop in that congregation. The term *episkopos*, originally synonymous with *presbyteros* or presbyter, now characterizes this distinctive office.[56] When the office of the monarchical bishop emerged, "one of its functions seems to have been winning pagans to the faith, although this was doubtless performed more energetically by some than by others."[57] In his letter to Polycarp, Ignatius encouraged him "'to exhort all men that they may be saved.' So, too, Gregory Thaumaturgos as Bishop was active in winning the pagans of his diocese."[58]

The fourth century witnessed a group of bishops who were scholars, theologians, and great preachers. In the East, the list included the following Greek fathers: Gregory of Nazianzus (390 CE), who became bishop of Constantinople, Basil the Great (370–79), who became bishop of Caesarea, and John Chrysostom of Antioch—"the Golden Mouth" (347–407), who ended up as archbishop of Constantinople. In the West, there were the Latin fathers that included Zeno (380), who became bishop of Verona, Ambrose (339–397), bishop of Milan, and Augustine, bishop of Hippo (334–430). The preaching of the church was considered to have reached the highest point of its ancient development especially through Chrysostom and Augustine in the fourth century.[59]

Chapter 13

The Sacraments

The term *sacrament* comes from the Latin word *sacramentum*, meaning an oath, as was taken by men joining the Roman army.[1] Pliny was the Roman governor of Bithynia, in Asia Minor. In writing to Emperor Trojan in Rome about 112 CE to report about the situation of Christians in his province, Pliny said:

> They maintained, however, that the amount of their fault or error had been this, that it was their habit on a fixed day to assemble before daylight and recite by turns a form of words to Christ as god, and that they bound themselves with an oath, not for any crime, but not to commit theft or robbery or adultery, not to break the word, and not to deny a deposit when demanded. After this was done, their custom was to depart, and to meet again to take food, but ordinary and harmless food; and even this (they said) they had given up doing after the issue of my edict by which in accordance with your commands I had forbidden the existence of clubs.[2]

By the time of the governor Pliny, the term *sacrament* was already used of Christian practices, and it was then that Pliny "misunderstood the Christians' sacraments to be oaths by which they promised not to commit crimes. The Latin Vulgate translated the Greek *mysterion* by *sacrament*, which led to Baptism and Eucharist being designated sacraments."[3] The practice of meeting together often led to new converts who were baptized there and then, and the breaking of bread together—all took place in the homes of the Christians. Therefore, for Christians, *sacrament* "is a rite in which is believed God's saving grace is uniquely active."[4] Grace means God's action in Christ Jesus. Methodists, along with the reformers, restricted the number of sacraments to two—baptism and the Eucharist, both mentioned in the New Testament (Matt. 28:19 and 1 Cor. 11:23–25), respectively.[5] The Roman Catholic Church has five additional sacraments that were added to the two "by the medieval Church."[6] These include confirmation, marriage, ordination, penance, and extreme unction.[7]

Baptism

First, "baptism marks the entry of the individual into the community of the church of Christ on earth."[8] Baptism is for both adults and children—that is, individuals can join the Christian community either through *believer's baptism* or *infant baptism*. Thus, "baptism is the initiation sacrament."[9] That is the reason in the Anglican tradition a baptismal font is placed at the entry of the church building. Second, theologically, "baptism is an action of God through his church. It is an action of God that is specific and personal, an action by which God claims a particular person into his victory through Jesus Christ."[10] Again, Baillie puts it correctly when he says: "In that sense our faith is a response to what God does for us first on Calvary and then in our baptism. *God's initiative precedes our faith; our faith follows.* Surely it is in subsequent faith going on right through a man's life that, above all, the sacrament becomes efficacious and a channel of the grace of God."[11] This is what Paul means when he writes, "Or don't you know that all of us who were baptized into Christ Jesus were baptized into his death? We were therefore buried with him through baptism into death in order that, just as Christ was raised from the dead through the glory of the Father, we too may live a new life" (Rom. 6:3–4).

In this whole activity, God uses human agencies: the minister places water on the new believer to be baptized, says the blessing of God, while the congregation proclaims the faith by taking the responsibility to nurture the individual in the Christian life.[12]

Third, regarding infant baptism: Why do we baptize children? (a) Historically, (i) as much as Jesus did not baptize, he welcomed children to come to him—the bearer of, and message of God's kingdom; and after receiving them in his arms, he "placed his hands on them and blessed them" (Mark 10:16). (ii) The phrase, "he/she and all his/her family were baptized," seems common in Paul's missionary journeys (Acts 16:15, 34). (iii) Jeremias quotes from Apostolic Tradition 21.4f, concerning the practice of baptism in North Africa in 220 CE: "First you should baptize the little ones. All who can speak for themselves should speak. But for those who cannot speak, their parents should speak, or another who belongs to the family. Then baptize the men, lastly the women."[13]

(b) Theologically, the Old Testament is the story of the "Old Covenant"—the covenant between God and the people of Israel, which was established by God's initiative after he had appeared to Abraham. God decided to bless Abraham and other nations through Abraham (Gen. 12:1–9). Therefore, he assured Abraham, "Do not be afraid, Abram. I am your shield" (Gen. 15:1); and "as sign of the covenant" (Gen. 17:11) or a seal to the covenant, God instructed Abraham that every male in his household who was eight years old (Gen. 17:12) should be circumcised (Gen. 17:10). This demand of the covenant included those who had been bought as slaves and foreigners in Abraham's household (Gen. 17:12–13). Abraham himself was ninety-nine years old when he was bound to that covenant initiated by God, and underwent the circumcision rite (Gen. 17:24). In that covenant, it was God's act of claiming Abraham to be his own, for reasons God alone knew—God's favor. It was an act of grace on the part of God, for Abraham had done nothing to deserve that favor. Circumcision symbolized or became the sign or seal of the covenant of God with a new community—the community of God. Oscar Cullman writes, "When heathen came over into Judaism, their children also were subjected along with them to the proselyte baptism."[14] He goes on to say, "The essence of the act of Baptism is the reception of a member into the divine covenant of grace of the Body of Christ, in whom the covenant with Abraham is fulfilled."[15]

The church, especially some churches in Africa, may want to ask, If the essence of the act of baptism is acknowledged as "the reception of a member into the divine covenant of grace of the Body of Christ," is there anything else that prevents a repentant person from receiving baptism? The answer is, nothing should stand in the way of a repentant sinner to attain baptism in the name of Christ (Acts 2:38). This was true of the Ethiopian eunuch (Acts 8:37).

Fourth, according to Hardin, Quillian, and White, who co-authored *The Celebration of the Gospel*, the three modes of baptism all symbolize God's action in the life of the individual in the name of the Father and of the Son and of the Holy Spirit:

(a) Immersion is the mode of baptism that most directly symbolizes union with Jesus Christ in his death and resurrection. In this mode one is put completely under the water and then brought out of the water. This act symbolically signifies the going down in death and being raised up into life—dying to the old self and living anew in Christ (Col. 3:3).

(b) Sprinkling symbolizes the cleansing from sins and the liberating from the *principle* of sin by the redeeming work of Jesus Christ. This awareness is caught up in the statement in John Wesley's Aldersgate testimony: "And an assurance was given me that he had taken away my sins, even mine, and saved me from the law of sin and death."[16]

(c) Baptism by pouring symbolizes the outpouring of the Holy Spirit—the "Lord and Giver of life" in the midst of the people, the Enlightener moving our minds to faith, and enabling us to say that Jesus Christ is Lord, the Comforter sustaining our hearts in hope.

Immersion, sprinkling, pouring—dying and rising with Christ, forgiveness, and the gift of the Holy Spirit—all are aspects of the work of

Jesus Christ in saving us from death to life. In fact, *each* mode is a way of understanding the *whole* work of Jesus Christ our Savior. The authors are correct in saying each mode of baptism participates in the meaning of the other two; so it does not matter which mode is used.[17]

Holy Communion

This sacrament goes by several names: the Holy Communion, the Holy Eucharist, the Lord's Supper, the Holy Liturgy, and the Mass. When I grew up in church, children were not allowed to partake in the Holy Communion. So we were always excused to leave the sanctuary, leaving the adults to partake. Time came when we were confirmed, which enabled us to participate.

Historically, the sacrament of the Holy Communion has its roots in: (a) the passion supper—which comes out of the Jewish Passover—when death struck the firstborn of Egypt, with God "passing over" the houses of the Hebrews (Exod. 12). Jesus gives new meaning to the Passover ceremony as he observed and partook the supper with his disciples. He took bread, blessed, broke, and gave it to his disciples as his body. He took a cup of wine, gave thanks, and passed it on to his disciples, calling it his blood of the new covenant (Matt. 26, Mark 14, Luke 22).[18]

(b) The resurrection supper—the disciples on the road to Emmaus recognized Jesus by breaking bread at the table, and knew he was risen (Luke 24:30–36). There is evidence that the early Christians were more mindful of the resurrection emphasis in the fellowship meal than they were of the passion-crucifixion emphasis (Acts 2:42–47, Acts 10:41, John 6, John 21, Rev. 3:30).[19] "It even appears that some of them were so overly exuberant in celebrating the resurrection meal that Paul had to remind them that the one who victoriously rose from the dead also was the one who sacrificially died for them and many (1 Cor. 11:17–24)."[20] Thus, "between the two suppers, the heart of the great redemptive act of in Christ had taken place—the passion-crucifixion-resurrection supper."[21]

The basic content of the Holy Communion regardless of the name used is as follows: First, Jesus commanded, "Do this in remembrance of me" (1 Cor. 11:24). This remembrance is not just a memorial of his death, but all that Jesus is to us now, including the whole creation, and as our hope that he is coming again.

Second, celebrating the Lord's Supper is at the same time proclamation. "For whenever you eat this bread and drink this cup, you proclaim the Lord's death until he comes," says Paul (1 Cor. 11:26).

Third, the offertory: "At the heart of the Christian faith is a mystery."[22] That mystery is Jesus Christ, to whom the scriptures and his church make their witness. Offertory is "that part of Holy Communion during which the Eucharistic bread and wine are being offered to God."[23] "One way to look at the whole meaning of the Holy Communion is as the celebration of the great double offertory—God's offering of himself to men through Christ; men offering of themselves to God through Christ."[24]

Fourth, participation: "Is not the cup of thanksgiving for which we give thanks a participation in the blood of Christ? And is not the bread that we break a participation in the body of Christ? Because there is one loaf, we, who are many, are one body, for we all share the one loaf" (1 Cor. 10:16–17). The heart of participation in the Holy Communion is Christ, through whom we are reconciled with God, our Father.

Fifth, thanksgiving: Many prayers of thanksgiving begin with the words, "Lift up your hearts." "It is thanksgiving for the great offertory, for the One remembered, for the proclaimed gospel, for participation in the death and resurrection and ascension of Jesus Christ."[25] That means the worshippers worship with joy and hope of participating in the Messianic banquet. Holy Communion is a celebration of God's redemptive work in Jesus Christ. The most depressing thing about sacraments in United Methodism in Africa is: (a) the sacraments do not receive attention that they deserve; and (b) the sacrament of the Holy Communion is more influenced by the cross-event (sadness or sorrow) than by the resurrection (victory, joy, celebration in the risen Christ).

Chapter 14

Eschatology

The term *eschatology* is derived from the Greek *eschatos*, meaning last or final, and means "the doctrine of the last things."[1] Biblical thought refers to the end of this evil age. Both the Old and the New Testaments view time in linear fashion; and both look forward to a consummation of history. Thus, eschatological elements and literature are found in both Judaism and Christianity.[2]

As a teaching method, it is often advisable to start from the known and move to the unknown or from your own context to that which is new. Thus, one might ask the question, What does African Religion teach about eschatology? A book co-authored by Professor John Mbiti made a scholarly contribution on the subject of eschatology, which included the following subheadings: African Eschatology, Christian Eschatology, and Attempt to Link Up African and Christian Eschatologies. Mbiti then discussed African Eschatology under the following subheadings: time, history, death and immortality, the after-life, and judgment.[3] In drawing his conclusion, one observation Mbiti rightly made was that "the concept of 'the end of the world' is both absent and meaningless in African traditional life and thought."[4]

The Ancestors or Ancestral Community

As much as the concept of the end of the world is both absent and meaningless in African traditional life and thought, the ancestors or ancestral community in the afterlife could be comparable to the concept of the end of the world in Judaism and Christianity. I shall share what African Religion teaches according to the Shona people of

Zimbabwe's traditional life and thought concerning their conception of the ancestors or ancestral community in the afterlife.

First, according to the Shona people's traditional life and thought, God, the Creator, created the human being as a corporate being of body and spirit; and while the physical body is mortal, the spirit, which is man's self, is immortal.

Second, they also believe that every individual being has a destiny; and that destiny is moving from the world of the mortals to that of the immortals, or moving from this realm we experience now into another realm of existence, where all the dead or living dead now reside—the realm of the ancestors, ancestral spirits, or ancestral community. The ancestral community is a gathering of all who died at an old age, those who died young, and both women and men. According to Shona traditional life and thought, at death the spirit of a married woman reverts to its parental ancestral community, and does not go to that of the husband. People in the ancestral community are gathered in one big family or clan community, as if they were still in this realm of existence. Pastor-teacher Jonas Manjengwa caught the vision of the traditional African ancestral community when he wrote a hymn to a typical African rhythm: "*Madzinza ariyo kunyika yaTenzi*" ("The clans are there in the world of the Lord"). Similarly, the author of the national anthem of the Republic of Zimbabwe caught the same vision when he wrote, "*Nyika yeMadzibaba neMadzitete*" ("The land of the fathers and great aunts" or the community of the fathers and the aunts).

There are two points I wish to lift as food for thought. One of the greatest yearnings in life whether one is in a happy marriage or not, especially for women, is to be united with one's blood family. The Shona traditional life and thought offers that opportunity once more to all women in the ancestral community. Reflect once more on Jesus' words of wisdom to the Sadducees concerning the issue of marriage: "Are you not in error because you do not know the Scriptures or the power of God? When the dead rise, they will neither marry nor be given in marriage; they will be like the angels in heaven" (Mark 12:24–25). African Religion, according to Shona traditional life and thought, always taught there was no more living in marriage in the ancestral community; rather, people live in big families or clans.

The second point is that according to Shona traditional life and thought "*Mazibaba* and *Madzitete*" refer to both genders exercising equal authority and powers. When it comes to resolving family conflict, *Madzitete* (aunts) have to be present. So it means there is equality of genders in the ancestral community.

Third, according to Shona traditional life and thought, for an individual to reach one's destiny—acceptance in the community of the ancestors—one has to develop a quality of life commonly understood as *unhu* or *hunhu*, or *ubunthu* while still in this life. A person who possesses *unhu* is one who "is well behaved, and is liked by other people . . . one who possesses good manners, good morals, good intelligence and knowledge."[5] Or *unhu* is that concept that says I am because I belong; it also means integrity. *Unhu* is developed in the context of family and community relations where one is because one belongs. *Unhu* dictates that one has to be a good person; and a good person is one who possesses *unhu*.

African Religion does not teach much about perfection. Rather, it teaches that any transgression should be made good either by showing that one is sorry in a tangible way or by offering an appropriate sacrifice.[6] People who are on the extreme opposite position of *unhu* in a community of the living are people considered as murderers and witches. Because in some of the Shona ethnic groups such persons are considered "enemies of life," they are buried separately from family cemeteries. Hence, there are no burial rituals for them, such as *tsvitsa* ritual, performed to a dead person after a year for purposes of commending the spirit of the deceased to the ancestors.

Acceptance into the ancestral community means one has reached his or her destiny. Again, for Shona traditional life and thought, that acceptance and incorporation into the ancestral community is salvation, the destiny of us all, where one finally finds rest. There is a common saying in Shona, "*Seka urema wafa.*" It literally means: "Laugh at the disability of another person only after your death." In other words, as long as one is still in this life one is still subject to dangers of evil. But once one is in the ancestral community, one is safe and one may laugh at anything. For salvation will have been secured. Another Shona saying that expresses a similar position of salvation and more of strength is "*Uchazondiona ndigere padombo.*" Literally, "You will see me sitting on a stone." Again, such an expression is often uttered by elderly persons who may feel they have been ignored or looked down upon, and as their way of fighting back say, "*Uchandiona ndigere padombo.*" *Dombo*—a stone symbolizes a position of strength, a position of power and influence, especially upon the life of the living. Thus, the elderly person would be saying, today in this life I may look old and feeble; but when I go to other side of the grave, I will fight back because I will be in a position of power and influence.

The spirits that are rejected from becoming part of the ancestral community end up returning to the realm of the living as demons, living in trees and mountain caves.

Fourth, the locus of the ancestors is not geographically distant from that of the living. Rather, the geographical loci of the two communities (the living and the ancestors) are intertwined. In making reference to the locus of the ancestors Mbiti says, "For the majority of the peoples, however, the next world is in fact geographically 'here', being separated from this only by virtue of being invisible to human beings."[7]

Shona traditional life and thought teaches that the locus of the ancestral community is closer to that of the Creator than to that of the living. Consequently, when a Shona person prays traditionally, the prayer is addressed to the ancestors. One does not close eyes or look up into space as if both the Creator and the ancestors are in a distant space; rather, one prays, uttering words as if in a conversation with another person sitting next to one. There is no shouting as if the ancestors do not hear; neither is the prayer long. Rather, the prayer is always to the point and short. The ancestors are "here" with us, they believe.

What is even more interesting for a theology student in Africa is that probably no other non-Christian teaching sheds light on the concept of the traditional doctrine of the communion of saints as "fellowship with holy people of all ages and the whole community of heaven"[8] as the African concept of the ancestral community. Through this African concept of the totality of the community, which includes both the living and the ancestral spirits, we can begin to understand the oneness of the church triumphant and church militant. John Parratt quoted E. Fashole-Luke saying, "We would suggest veneration of our ancestors in Africa and our passionate desire to be linked with our dead in a real and genuine way can be satisfied by the development of a sound doctrine of the communion of saints" ("Ancestor Veneration" 220).[9]

Further, "in the Eastern Church it seems to have meant originally 'the participation in holy things,' i.e. the *eucharist*, but the more usual understanding of 'communion with the departed saints' is also attested quite early: see Kelly's discussion (J. N. D. Kelly, *Early Christian Creeds* (London: 1972), 388ff."[10]

The Old Testament and Eschatology

For Judaism, history begins with the Patriarchs. Then came deliverance from Egypt, the settlement in the Promised Land, and the government as a *theocracy*—a rule of the state by God, or a government of a state by priests or clergy. Change came with Saul after Israel asked for a king (1 Sam. 8:1ff), then the Davidic Rule (1 Sam. 16:1ff). From Solomon's rule, the kingdom is divided between Jeroboam, one of Solomon's officials in the North, the Kingdom of Israel, and Rehoboam, a son of Solomon in the South, the Kingdom of Judah. The northern kingdom of Israel is destroyed by Assyria (2 Kings 17:7ff) in about 930 BCE.

In spite of the division of Israel that caused the northern and southern kingdoms, and the ensuing destruction of the northern kingdom by the Assyrians, the consistent rule of the southern kingdom by other nations led the Israelites to always believe they were a chosen people, and that one day God would intervene on their behalf. From the eighth to the fifth centuries, the prophets had proved champions in the history of Israel by proclaiming the will of God in spite of the harsh and humiliating political and economic conditions they suffered. William Barclay declares that if we are going to understand the concept of the second coming of Christ, we need to understand that its whole background is in the Old Testament. The eighth-century Old Testament prophets began proclaiming the Day of the Lord, which would come and was experienced in the history of Israel. The Israelites then divided time into ages. There was the present age that was considered bad, and there was the age to come that would be considered the golden age of God. The Day of the Lord was located in between the two ages—and it was the most terrible day.[11] Amos rebuked Israel for desiring to see the Day of the Lord, which would be a day of darkness (Amos 5:18–20). Similarly, several other prophets of the Old Testament also portrayed the Day of the Lord as a terrible day (Isa. 22:5, 13:9, Zeph. 1:14–16, Jer. 30:7, Mal. 4:1, Joel 2:31).

With the harsh and oppressive experience of the Babylonian Exile (586 BCE), Israel began looking both backward in her history and forward to new expectations: (1) Backward they looked to the "ideal Davidic kingdom" of the past, which became the hope for the future; and (2) forward with eschatological expectations—the hope for a messianic ruler of the House of David (Isa. 9:2ff, 11:1ff). In later Judaism, there appeared the concept of "the Son of man," and this title does not refer to a human being, but rather to an exalted being (Dan. 7:13ff).[12]

> In late Judaism two hopes ran parallel: the first affirmed the coming of the Messiah and the inauguration of the

> Davidic kingdom; the second looked for the Son of man, a supernatural agent, to come on the clouds of heaven and to inaugurate the new age. This two-age view of history is what we find in the New Testament period, except perhaps in the Gospel of John, where it has been largely replaced by a special view of two orders of reality, the world above and the world below.[13]

Another scholar put it this way:

> By the time of the New Testament, different Jews had different understandings of what the future ruler would be like. Some expected a warrior-king like David, others a more supernatural cosmic judge of the earth, and still others (such as the community that produced the Dead Sea Scrolls) a priestly ruler who would provide the authoritative interpretations of God's law for the people.[14]

The New Testament and Eschatology

On the basis of the Gospel tradition, Jesus used the term "the Son of man" in the eschatological manner. "It is not likely . . . that Jesus used the term of himself, but rather of the exalted Son of man who would soon come in judgment and to establish God's kingdom."[15]

The early church evangelized the Roman Empire at a time when the issue of the *parousia* of Christ was considered imminent. The Greek word *parousia* means "a being present, presence (1 Cor. 16:17, 2 Cor. 10:10) . . . a coming, arrival, advent (2 Cor. 7:6, 7, Phil. 1:26, 2 Thess. 2:9)."[16] "Paul speaks of his *parousia* in Philippi, Phil. 2:12 (in contrast to his *apousia*, his absence)."[17] However, the New Testament speaks specifically "of the *Advent* or *Parousia* of Christ (Matt. 24:3, 27, 37, 39, 1 Cor. 15:23, 1 Thess. 2:19, 3:13, 4:15, 5:23, 2 Thess. 2:1, 8, James 5:7, 8, 2 Pet. 1:16, 3:4, 12, 1 John 2:28).[18] The early church entertained a strong belief in the immediate second coming of Christ. They expected the *parousia* of Christ in their lifetime, and it had been delayed. Scoffers taunted the Christians saying, "Where is this 'coming' he promised?" (2 Pet. 3:4). Further, it appeared some of the Thessalonians had misunderstood Paul and thought all the believers would live until the *parousia* of Christ. That was what raised the question concerning those believers who had since passed on: Would they be part of the great day when Christ comes (1 Thess. 4:13)? They wondered what would become of them, for they also, like the ten virgins, were waiting to meet the bridegroom (Matt. 25:1) in their lifetime. Paul believed in educating the congregations he founded, and he took that challenge as an opportunity to teach the believers in Thessalonica about the Christian attitude in the face of death. He challenged the believers not to grieve over their dead "like the rest of mankind, who have no hope" (1 Thess. 4:13). William Barclay shared the attitude of some people in the pagan world when faced by death—how they stood in despair; and that they met death with grim resignation and total hopelessness. Thus he shared some examples of testimonies of such persons of the pagan world:

> Aeschylus wrote, "Once a man dies there is no resurrection." Theocritus wrote, "There is hope for those who are alive, but those who have died are without hope." Catullus wrote, "When once our brief light sets, there is one perpetual night through which we must sleep." On their tombstones grim epitaphs were carved. "I was not; I became; I am not; I care not."[19]

Paul assured the believers that the glory of that day, which was soon to come, would be shared by all—all who died in Christ, and those who were still alive. Thus, he emphasized the gospel in which he believed, "We believe Jesus died and rose again, and so we believe that God will bring with Jesus those who have fallen asleep in him" (1 Thess. 4:14).

The main issue Paul is making to the believers in Thessalonica is that a person who dies in Christ and a person who is still now living and in Christ, are all in Christ. All have their hope in the living Christ who conquered death; and both will participate in the glorious day of his coming again (1 Thess. 4:13–18).

In spite of all the misconceptions related to the *parousia* of Christ, the delayed *parousia* of Christ gave the early Christians the opportunity to evangelise because they continued believing in his coming even in the imminent eschatology—the belief that Jesus would soon appear. Thus, they encouraged one another and built each other up (1 Thess. 5:11) through the preaching of the Word so that when the Lord appeared, they would be confident and unashamed before him (1 John 2:28). It is the message of which William Abraham writes, "Evangelism in the early church was rooted in the eschatological activity of God, which was inaugurated in the life, death and resurrection of Jesus of Nazareth and continued in the acts of the Holy Spirit."[20]

Indeed the *parousia* of Christ is delayed, but it is coming, and it remains imminent. This continues to be the evangelical message of the Church of Jesus Christ to the world.

The teaching of the *parousia* enables the church of Christ not to be found napping, as was the case with the five foolish virgins in the parable of the ten virgins (Matt. 25:1–13). This same message of the *parousia* is presented in the parables of the talents (Matt. 25:14–30) and "the sheep and the goats" (Matt. 25:31–46). There is a great misconception about the message of the *parousia* by some Christians. These Christians believe that they exist as a church primarily to prepare to go to heaven or only to wait for Jesus to come. A study of the three parables in Matthew 25 (the ten virgins, the talents, and the sheep and the goats) shows that while the parables are about waiting, such waiting does not mean Christians are in a period of inactivity or idleness.

The church of Christ on earth could be pockets of the kingdom of God where God's love is experienced by those who need love, where those who need to be comforted receive comfort, and where people die in the lap of someone who loves them, rather than dying alone. This is all within the spirit of the message of the *parousia*, and that is why Jesus prayed, "My prayer is not that you take them out of the world but that you protect them from the evil one" (John 17:15).

Each time the church of Christ meets to celebrate the gospel, it must display God's mission as its agenda and evangelism as a priority. As much as the church knows that the Lord is coming again, the Lord expects to find his church involved in his Father's mission. There is no better way for the church of Christ to prepare itself to meet the Lord unashamedly than to continue with the unfinished mission of Christ on earth.

Notes

Chapter 1: What Is Theology?

1. G. Abbott-Smith, *A Manual Greek Lexicon of the New Testament* (Edinburgh: T. & T. Clark, 1968), 205.
2. Ibid.
3. J. Sherrell Hendricks, Gene E. Sease, Eric Lane Titus, James Bryan Wiggins, *Christian Word Book* (Nashville: Abingdon Press, 1968), 298.
4. John Macquarrie, *Principles of Christian Theology*, rev. ed. (London: SCM Press LTD, 1977), 1.
5. L. Harold DeWolf, *A Theology of the Living Church* (New York: Harper & Row Brothers, 1953), 18.
6. Daniel L. Migliore, *Faith Seeking Understanding* (Grand Rapids: William B. Eerdmans, 2001), 2.
7. Philip S. Watson, "Outline of Theology I" (Class Notes, 1965).
8. Hendricks et al., *Christian Word Book*, 111.
9. W. E. Vine, *An Expository Dictionary of the New Testament Words*, Vol. I (Old Tappan, NJ: Fleming H. Revell, 1966), 331.
10. Barclay M. Newman Jr., *Greek-English Dictionary of the New Testament* (London: United Bible Societies, 1971), 45.
11. Hendricks et al., *Christian Word Book*, 82.
12. Marcus Ward, *The Outlines of Christian Doctrine*, Vol. 1 (Madras: The Christian Literature Society, 1966), 1.
13. J. F. Bethune-Baker, *An Introduction to the Early History of Christian Doctrine* (London: Methuen & Co., 1949), 1.
14. Vincent Taylor, *Doctrine and Evangelism* (London: The Epworth Press, 1953), 7.
15. Philip Watson, *The Concept of Grace* (Philadelphia: Muhlenberg Press, 1959), 62f.
16. Ibid., 63.
17. Ibid.
18. Macquarrie, *Principles of Christian Theology*, 4.
19. Ibid.
20. Lovett H. Weems, Jr., *John Wesley's Message Today* (Nashville: Abingdon Press, 1982), 13.
21. Ibid., 5
22. Van A. Harvey, *A Handbook of Theological Terms* (New York: The Macmillan Company, 1964), 207.

23. John Baillie, *The Idea of Revelation in Recent Thought* (New York: Columbia University Press, 1956), 19.
24. Harvey, *A Handbook of Theological Terms*, 207.
25. Ibid.
26. Baillie, *The Idea of Revelation in Recent Thought*, 33.
27. DeWolf, *A Theology of the Living Church*, 67.
28. Alan Richardson, ed., *A Theological Word Book of the Bible* (New York: The Macmillan Company, 1966).
29. Dwight E. Stevenson, *In the Biblical Preacher's Workshop* (Nashville: Abingdon Press, 1967), 18.
30. Macquarrie, *Principles of Christian Theology*, 11.
31. Ibid.
32. Ibid., 11.
33. Migliore, *Faith Seeking Understanding*, 9.
34. Macquarrie, *Principles of Christian Theology*, 39.
35. Ibid., 40
36. Ibid.
37. Ibid.
38. Migliore, *Faith Seeking Understanding*, 9.
39. Macquarrie, *Principles of Christian Theology*, 39.
40. Ibid.
41. Migliore, *Faith Seeking Understanding*, 2.
42. DeWolf, *A Theology of the Living Church*, 18.
43. Gustaf Aulen, *The Faith of the Christian Church* (Philadelphia: The Muhlenberg Press, 1962), 2.
44. Paul Tillich, *Systematic Theology*, Vol. I (Chicago: University of Chicago Press, 1951), 3.
45. Ibid.
46. Macquarrie, *Principles of Christian Theology*, 33f.
47. Tillich, *Systematic Theology*, Vol. 1, 60f.
48. Migliore, *Faith Seeking Understanding*, 14.
49. Ward, *The Outlines of Christian Doctrine*, Vol. 1, xi
50. *Black World* (August 1971): 75.
51. Paul Planton, "Phenomenology of Religion, Fall 1971" (Class Notes).
52. *Journal of Theology for Southern Africa* 11 (July 1975): 32.

Chapter 2: The Making of the Bible

1. Norman K. Gottwald, *A Light to the Nations* (New York: Harper & Row, 1959), 2.
2. "Most students would be accustomed to dating ancient events as either A.D. (which does not stand for 'After Death,' but for *'anno domini,'* Latin for 'year of our Lord') or B.C. ('Before Christ'). This terminology may make sense for Christians, for whom A.D. 2002 is indeed 'the year of our Lord.' It makes less sense, though, for Jews, Muslims, and others for whom Jesus is not the 'Lord' or the 'Christ.' Scholars have therefore begun to use a different set of abbreviations as more

inclusive of others outside the Christian tradition. In this book I will follow the alternative designations of CE (the Common Era, meaning common to people of all faiths who utilize the western calendar) and BCE (Before the Common Era). In terms of the older abbreviations, then, CE corresponds to A.D. and BCE to B.C." Bart D. Ehrman, *The New Testament: A Historical Introduction to the Early Christian Writings*, 2nd ed. (Oxford: Oxford University Press, 2000), 8.
3. Harrell F. Beck, *Our Biblical Heritage* (Boston: United Church Press, 1964), 23.
4. C. H. Dodd, *The Bible Today* (Cambridge: Cambridge University Press, 1962), 33f.
5. Ehrman, *The New Testament*, 2nd ed., 2.
6. W. R. Browning, *A Dictionary of the Bible* (Oxford: Oxford University Press, 1996), 57.
7. Bernhard W. Anderson, *The Living World of the Old Testament*, 2nd ed. (London: Lowe & Brydone Printers Ltd., 1967), 286.
8. Ibid., 289.
9. Ibid., 288.
10. "Introduction, Micah," *The NIV Study Bible*, 1363.
11. Anderson, *The Living World of the Old Testament*, 289.
12. Ibid., 291.
13. Ibid., 375.
14. Beck, *Our Biblical Heritage*, 34.
15. Browning, *A Dictionary of the Bible*, 288.
16. Beck, *Our Biblical Heritage*, 24.
17. Ibid., 24.
18. Ibid.
19. Ibid.
20. Ibid.
21. Ehrman, *The New Testament*, 8.
22. Ibid.
23. Adolf Von Harnack, *The Origin of the New Testament* (Covent Garden: Williams and Norgate, 1925), 8.
24. Kenneth Scott Latourette, *History of Christianity*, rev. ed. (San Francisco: Harper Collins Publishers, 1975), 125.
25. Werner Georg Kummel, *Introduction to the New Testament*, trans. A. J. Mattill, Jr. (Nashville: Abingdon Press, 1966), 342.
26. Ibid., 345.
27. Ibid.
28. Ibid.
29. Richardson, ed., *A Theological Word Book of the Bible*, 156.
30. Beck, *Our Biblical Heritage*, 13.
31. Ibid.
32. Vine, *An Expository Dictionary of New Testament Words*, Vol. II, 263.
33. J. N. D. Kelly, *A Commentary on The Pastoral Epistles: I Timothy, II Timothy, Titus* (New York: Harper & Row Publishers, 1963), 203.
34. Migliore, *Faith Seeking Understanding*, 43.

35. Ibid., 44.
36. Kelly, A *Commentary of the Pastoral Epistles*, 203.
37. Bruce Metzger, *The Canon of the New Testament* (Oxford: Clarendon Press, 1987), 254.
38. DeWolf, A *Theology of the Living Church*, 76.
39. Macquarrie, *Principles of Christian Theology*, 280.
40. Beck, *Our Biblical Heritage*, 14ff.
41. Migliore, *Faith Seeking Understanding*, 46.
42. G. Ernest Wright and Reginald Fuller, *The Book of the Acts of God* (Harmondsworth: Penguin Books Ltd, 1960), 18f.
43. Ibid., 22.
44. Richardson, ed., A *Theological Word Book of the Bible*, 131.
45. *The Interpreter's Dictionary of the Bible*, Vol. R–Z (Nashville: Abingdon Press, 1962), 251.
46. Jean-Jacques van Allmen, *Preaching and Congregation* (Richmond: John Knox Press, 1962), 7.

Chapter 3: Belief in God

1. *Collins Concise Dictionary of the English Language* (London: William Collins Sons & Co. Ltd. 1978), 349.
2. John Wesley Zwomunondiita Kurewa, *African Religion: The Quarry of the Rock of Monotheism* (Nashville: Discipleship Resources, 2013), 28f.
3. *The Interpreter's Bible*, Vol. VI (1956), 848.
4. Bruce Manning Metzger, *The New Testament: Its Background, Growth, and Content* (Nashville: Abingdon Press, 1965), 184
5. E. Bolaji Idowu, *African Traditional Religion* (London: SCM Press, 1973), 140.
6. Ibid., 149.
7. Ibid.
8. Ibid., 152.
9. Ibid.
10. Ibid., 155.
11. Ibid.
12. Ibid., 161.
13. Ibid., 165.
14. Gabriel Setiloane, *The Image of God Among the Sotho-Tswana* (Rotterdam: A. A. Balkema, 1976), 33.
15. Ibid., 34.
16. Warren C. Young, A *Christian Approach to Philosophy* (Grand Rapids: Baker Book House, 1954), 249.
17. Dagobert D. Runes, ed., *Dictionary of Philosophy* (Totowa, NJ: Littlefield, Adams & Co., 1971), 205f.
18. Ward, *The Outlines of Christian Doctrine*, Vol. 2, 5.
19. Runes, ed., *Dictionary of Philosophy*, 131f.
20. *Collins Concise Dictionary of the English Language*, 367.

21. Ward, *The Outlines of Christian Doctrine*, Vol. 2, 7.
22. Kenneth D. Kaunda, *A Humanist in Africa* (Nashville: Abingdon Press, 1966), 39.
23. Ibid., 8.
24. "The Apostles' Creed, Ecumenical Version," par. 882, *The United Methodist Hymnal* (Nashville: Abingdon Press, 1989).
25. Ward, *The Outlines of Christian Doctrine*, Vol. 1, 1.
26. Ward, *The Outlines of Christian Doctrine*, Vol. 1, 4.
27. Gerhard Von Rad, *Old Testament Theology*, Vol. I (New York: Harper & Row, 1957), 140.
28. Harrell F. Beck, *Our Biblical Heritage* (Boston: United Church Press, 1964), 36.
29. Ibid.
30. Ibid., 38.
31. Von Rad, *Old Testament Theology*, 141.
32. Jurgen Moltmann, *God in Creation*, 2nd ed. (London: SCM Press, 1989), 217.
33. Charles F. Kraft, *Genesis* (New York: Women's Division of Christian Service Board of Missions, The Methodist Church, 1964), 38.
34. Ibid., 44.
35. Ibid., 45.
36. Migliore, *Faith Seeking Understanding*, 126.
37. *The Works of John Wesley*, Vol. 9, 269.
38. *The Works of John Wesley*, Vol. 6, 66.
39. Ibid., 66.
40. Ibid., 270.
41. Migliore, *Faith Seeking Understanding*, 122.
42. Moltmann, *God in Creation*, 217.
43. Hendricks et al., *Christian Word Book*, 34.
44. *Collins Concise Dictionary of the English Language*, 46.
45. W. R. F. Browning, *A Dictionary of the Bible* (Oxford: Oxford University Press, 1966), 174.
46. Walter Klaiber, "Scriptural Holiness," *Proceedings of the Fifteenth World Methodist Conference* (1986): 85.
47. Ibid.
48. Browning, *A Dictionary of the Bible*, 174.
49. Von Rad, *Old Testament Theology*, 199.
50. Vine, *An Expository Dictionary of NT Words*, 298.
51. DeWolf, *A Theology of the Living Church*, 114.
52. Von Rad, *Old Testament Theology*, 370.
53. Ibid., 96.
54. DeWolf, *A Theology of the Living Church*, 108.
55. Ibid., 117.
56. Ibid., 118f.
57. Ibid., 121.
58. Ibid., 114.
59. Vine, *An Expository Dictionary of New Testament Words*, Vol. 2, 132.

Chapter 4: Humanity and Sin

1. Mircea Eliade, ed., *The Encyclopedia of Religion*, Vol. 1 (New York: Macmillan, 1987), 71.
2. Ibid.
3. Laurenti Magesa, *African Religion* (New York: Orbis Books, 1997), 161.
4. *The* NIV *Study Bible Footnotes*, 9.
5. Ibid.
6. Kraft, *Genesis*, 47.
7. *The* NIV *Study Bible Footnotes*, 9.
8. *The Works of John Wesley*, Vol. 6, 67.
9. Ibid., 67.
10. Ibid.
11. Ibid., 67f.
12. Ibid., 50.
13. *The Works of John Wesley*, Vol. 9, 456.
14. *The Works of John Wesley*, Vol. 9, 456.
15. *The Works of John Wesley*, Vol. 6, 58.
16. Harvey, *A Handbook of Theological Terms*, 220.
17. Henry Bettenson, *The Later Christian Fathers* (London: Oxford University Press, 1970), 196.
18. Hendricks et al., *Christian Word Book*, 280.
19. Migliore, *Faith Seeking Understanding*, 135.
20. Greville P. Lewis, ed., *An Approach to Christian Doctrine* (London: The Epworth Press, 1957), 59.
21. Ibid., 59ff.
22. Richardson, ed., *A Theological Word Book of the Bible*, 227.
23. Ibid.
24. Ibid.
25. Ibid.
26. Harvey, *A Handbook of Theological Terms*, 221.
27. Ibid.
28. Ibid.
29. Migliore, *Faith Seeking Understanding*, 122.

Chapter 5: Evil and the Providence of God

1. Hendricks et al., *Christian Word Book*, 298.
2. *Webster's New World Dictionary* (Cleveland: The World Publishing Company, 1956), 504.
3. DeWolf, *A Theology of the Living Church*, 278.
4. Ward, *The Outlines of Christian Doctrine*, Vol. 1, 200.
5. Ibid.
6. Footnote, Matt. 13:25, *The* NIV *Study Bible*, 1458.

7. Ward, *The Outlines of Christian Doctrine*, Vol. 1, 204.
8. Migliore, *Faith Seeking Understanding*, 101.
9. Ibid., 202.
10. Ibid.
11. Ibid., 202
12. Ibid.
13. Ibid.
14. Ibid., 203.
15. Ward, *The Outlines of Christian Doctrine*, Vol. 1, 205.
16. *The Interpreter's Dictionary of the Bible*, Vol. R–Z, 225.
17. Ward, *The Outlines of Christian Doctrine*, Vol. 1, 206.
18. Francis Wright Beare, *The Gospel According to Matthew* (San Francisco: Harper & Row, 1981), 107.
19. Ward, *The Outlines of Christian Doctrine*, Vol. 1, 206.
20. *The Interpreter's Dictionary of the Bible*, Vol. R–Z, 225.
21. Ward, *The Outlines of Christian Doctrine*, Vol. 1, 207.
22. Beare, *The Gospel According to Matthew*, 107.
23. Hendricks et al., *Christian Word Book*, 242.
24. Paul J. Glenn, *The History of Philosophy* (London: B. Herder Book Co., 1959), 106.
25. Hendricks et al., *Christian Word Book*, 242.
26. Ibid.
27. *Oxford Dictionary of the Bible*, 306.
28. Migliore, *Faith Seeking Understanding*, 100.

Chapter 6: Christology

1. Lewis, ed., *An Approach to Christian Doctrine*, 94.
2. Ibid.
3. Harvey, *A Handbook of Theological Terms*, 48.
4. Ehrman, *The New Testament*, 61.
5. Ibid.
6. Hendricks et al., *Christian Word Book*, 287.
7. Gunther Bornkamm, *Jesus of Nazareth* (New York: Harper & Row, 1960), 56.
8. Ibid., 57.
9. Beare, *The Gospel According to Matthew*, 70.
10. Ibid.
11. Hendricks et al., *Christian Word Book*, 313.
12. Ibid., 254.
13. Ibid.
14. Ibid.
15. Harvey, *A Handbook of Theological Terms*, 40.
16. Browning, *A Dictionary of the Bible*, 63.
17. John Parratt, *Reinventing Christianity: African Theology Today* (Grand Rapids: William B. Eerdmans, 1995), 175.

18. Malcolm J. McVeigh, "*Salvation in the African Context*," 4.
19. Magesa, *African Religion: The Moral Traditions of Abundant Life*, 161.
20. Ibid.
21. Ibid.
22. *Collins Concise Dictionary of the English Language*, 602.

Chapter 7: The Holy Spirit

1. *The United Methodist Hymnal: Book of United Methodist Worship* (Nashville: The Methodist Publishing House, 1989), 880.
2. DeWolf, *A Theology of the Living Church*, 270.
3. Browning, *A Dictionary of the Bible*, 352.
4. Ibid., 174.
5. William Barclay, *The Promise of the Spirit* (London: The Epworth Press, 1960), 12ff.
6. Ibid., 32.
7. William Barclay, *The Acts of the Apostles*, rev. ed. (Philadelphia: Westminster Press, 1976), 21.
8. Browning, *A Dictionary of the Bible*, 134.
9. Barclay, *The Acts of the Apostles*, 21.
10. Ibid., 95.
11. F. F. Bruce, *Commentary on the Book of the Acts* (Grand Rapids: William B. Eerdmans, 1966), 55f.
12. Frederick Dale Bruner, *A Theology of the Holy Spirit* (Grand Rapids: William B. Eerdmans, 1970), 162.
13. Ibid.
14. Ibid.
15. C. S. C. Williams, *A Commentary on the Acts of the Apostles* (New York: Harper & Row, 1957), 62.
16. Ibid., 62.
17. Richard Belward Rackham, *The Acts of the Apostles* (London: Methuen & Co., 1930), 17.
18. Bruner, *A Theology of the Holy Spirit*, 163.
19. Ibid., 161.
20. Bruce, *Commentary on the Book of Acts*, 63.
21. Ibid., 59.
22. Bruner, *A Theology of the Holy Spirit*, 164.
23. According to Bruce, "The real sense of Exod. 20:18 is made clear in ARV: "All the people perceived thundering" (*Ibid.*).
24. Ibid., 59f.
25. Footnotes, John 14:18, *The NIV Study Bible*, 1622.
26. Footnotes, John 16:13, *The NIV Study Bible*, 1625.
27. Bruce, *Commentary on the Book of the Acts*, 77.
28. Aulen, *The Faith of the Christian Church*, 221.

29. Merrill C. Tenney, *John: The Gospel of Belief* (Grand Rapids: William B. Eerdmans, 1948), 220.
30. Bruce, *Commentary on the Book of the Acts*, 78.

Chapter 8: The Holy Trinity

1. Browning, *A Dictionary of the Bible*, 379.
2. *The Interpreter's Dictionary of the Bible*, Vol. R–Z, 711.
3. Footnotes, Mark 12:29, *The NIV Study Bible*, 1517.
4. Ibid.
5. J. L. Neve, *A History of Christian Thought*, Vol. 1 (1946), 106.
6. Bruce Manning Metzger, *The New Testament: Its Background, Growth, and Content* (Nashville: Abingdon Press, 1965), 179f.
7. DeWolf, *A Theology of the Living Church*, 278.
8. Ibid.
9. DeWolf, *A Theology of the Living Church*, 278.
10. Tillich, *A History of Christian Thought*, 46.
11. Ibid.
12. Ibid.
13. *The Interpreter's Dictionary of the Bible*, 711.
14. Ward, *The Outlines of Christian Doctrine*, Vol. 1, 190.
15. DeWolf, *A Theology of the Living Church*, 274.
16. Aulen, *The Faith of the Christian Church*, 225.
17. J. L. Neve, *A History of Christian Thought* (Philadelphia: Fortress Press, 1946), 51.
18. Harvey, *A Handbook of Theological Terms*, 45.
19. Ibid., 106.
20. Ibid., 121.
21. Tillich, *A History of Christian Thought*, 46.
22. Ibid., 78.
23. Neve, *A History of Christian Thought*, 108.
24. Cave, *The Doctrine of the Person of Christ*, 97.
25. Tillich, *A History of Christian Thought*, 70.
26. Neve, *A History of Christian Thought*, Vol. 1, 109.
27. Neve, *A History of Christian Thought*, 109.
28. Collins Concise Dictionary of the English Language.
29. Cave, *The Doctrine of the Person of Christ*, 103.
30. Ibid.
31. Ibid., 117.
32. J. N. D. Kelly, *Early Christian Doctrines*, 2nd ed. (New York: Harper & Row, Publishers, 1960), 238.
33. Tillich, *A History of Christian Thought*, 75.
34. Ibid., 77.
35. Ibid., 71.
36. Ibid.

37. Ibid.
38. Ibid.
39. Ibid., 71f.
40. Ibid., 77.

Chapter 9: The Atonement

1. *Collins Concise Dictionary of the English Language*, 45.
2. Ibid.
3. Hendricks et al., *Christian Word Book*, 32.
4. Harvey, *A Handbook of Theology*, 33.
5. Browning, *A Dictionary of the Bible*, 29.
6. S. E. M. Pheko, *African Religion Rediscovered* (Bulawayo: Daystar Publications, 1965), 17.
7. Ibid.
8. William E. Hordern, *A Layman's Guide to Protestant Theology* (London: The Macmillan Company, 1968), 25.
9. Taylor, *Doctrine and Evangelism*, 43.
10. Ibid.
11. Ibid., 43f.
12. Hendricks et al., *Christian Word Book*, 33.
13. Hordern, *A Layman's Guide to Protestant Theology*, 26.
14. Hendricks et al., *Christian Word Book*, 33.
15. Hordern, *A Layman's Guide to Protestant Theology*, 26.
16. Migliore, *Faith Seeking Understanding*, 152.
17. *Document of the Christian Church*, 2nd ed., 138.
18. Hendricks et al., *Christian Word Book*, 33.
19. Hordern, *A Layman's Guide to Protestant Theology*, 26f.
20. Gustaf Aulen, *Christus Victor* (New York: The Macmillan Company, 1969), 2.
21. Hordern, *A Layman's Guide to Protestant Theology*, 28.
22. Isaac Watts, "When I Survey the Wondrous Cross" (1707), p.d.
23. *Long Walk to Freedom: The Autobiography of Nelson Mandela* (Randburg: Macdonald Purnell [PVY] Ltd., 1994), 370.

Chapter 10: The Church

1. *Official Journal: Minutes of the First Session of the Rhodesia Mission Conference of the Methodist Episcopal Church* (1916), 60.
2. *Official Journal: Minutes of the Second and Third Sessions of the Rhodesia Mission Conference of the Methodist Episcopal Church* (1917), 50.
3. Vine, *An Expository Dictionary of New Testament Words*, 294.
4. R. Newton Flew, *Jesus and His Church* (London: Epworth Press, 1960), 20.
5. Ibid., 25.
6. Ibid., 21.
7. DeWolf, *A Theology of the Living Church*, 299.
8. Browning, *A Dictionary of the Bible*, 76.

9. Ward, *The Outlines of Christian Doctrine*, Vol. 2, 84.
10. Flew, *Jesus and His Church*, 24.
11. Hendricks et al., *Christian Word Book*, 51.
12. Alan Richardson, *An Introduction to the Theology of the New Testament* (n.p.: n.d.), 266.
13. Lewis, ed., *An Approach to Christian Doctrine*, 159.
14. Ibid.
15. Ibid.
16. Ibid., 160.
17. Ibid.
18. Ibid.
19. Aulen, *The Faith of the Christian Church*, 293f.
20. C. H. Dodd, *The Apostolic Preaching and Its Development* (New York: Harper & Row, Publishers, 1964), 21.
21. Aulen, *The Faith of the Christian Church*, 294.
22. Metzger, *The New Testament: Its Background, Growth, and Content*, 179.
23. Bruce, *Commentary on the Book of the Acts*, 56.
24. Lewis, ed., *An Approach to Christian Doctrine*, 163.
25. Aulen, *The Faith of the Christian Church*, 299.
26. Aulen, *The Faith of the Christian Church*, 305.
27. Norman Goodall, *The Ecumenical Movement*, 2nd ed. (London: Oxford University Press, 1966), 3.
28. *Handbook of Christian Theology* (Cleveland: World Publishing Company, 1969), 57.

Chapter 11: The Church and God's Mission

1. Theodore H. Robinson, *The Moffatt Commentary of Matthew* (New York: Harper & Row Publishers, 1927), 236.
2. David H. Stern, *Amen Complete Jewish Bible* (Clarksville, MD: Jewish New Testament Publications, 1998), 1230.
3. Footnotes, 2 Cor. 12:9, *The NIV Study Bible*, 1777.
4. Oscar Cullmann, *Prayer in the New Testament* (Minneapolis: Fortress Press, 1995), xiv.
5. W. E. Sangster, *Teach Me to Pray* (Nashville: Upper Room Books, 1959), 36f.
6. W. E. Sangster, *The Craft of Sermon Construction* (Philadelphia: Westminster Press, 1951), 53.
7. Gordon Pratt Baker and Edward Ferguson, Jr., eds., "How to Give an Altar Call in a Local Church," *A Year of Evangelism in the Local Church* (Nashville: Tidings Materials for Christian Evangelism, 1960), 72.
8. *The Financial Gazette* (2–8 December 2010): A3-A5.
9. Beck, *Our Biblical Heritage*, 2.
10. Davies, *Methodism*, 73.
11. *Foundations: Sharing the Ministry of Christian Education in Your Congregation* (n.p.: 1993), 4.

12. Thomas D. Blakely, Walter E. A. van Beek, Dennis L. Thomson, eds., *Religion in Africa* (London: James Currey, 1994), 280.
13. Richardson, ed., *A Theological Word Book of the Bible*, 103.
14. Ibid.
15. Ibid.
16. Kathy Black, *A Healing Homiletic* (Nashville: Abingdon Press, 1996), 51.
17. Ibid.
18. Ibid.
19. Ibid., 17.
20. "The Mission Extension of the United Methodist Church in Africa," *Umbowo* (October 1972): 5.
21. "Empirical Medicine in the 18th Century: The Rev. John Wesley's Search for Remedies that Work," *Methodist History* 44:4 (July 2006): 217.
22. Ibid., 217f.
23. *The Works of John Wesley*, Vol. XIV, 307.
24. Ibid., 309.
25. Ibid., 310.

Chapter 12: Historical Development of the Ministry

1. C. K. Barrett, *The Signs of an Apostle* (Philadelphia: Fortress Press, 1969), 45.
2. Vine, *An Expository Dictionary of New Testament Words*, 63.
3. Ibid.
4. A. G. Herbert, *Apostle and Bishop* (New York: Seabury Press, 1963), 42.
5. Bultmann, *Theology of the New Testament*, Vol. 1, 58f.
6. C. K. Barrett, *A Commentary on the First Epistle to the Corinthians* (London: Adam and Charles Black, 1968), 5.
7. Metzger, *The New Testament*, 180.
8. Charles M. Laymon, ed., *The Interpreter's One-Volume Commentary on the Bible* (Nashville: Abingdon Press, 1971), 835.
9. Richard Belward Rackham, *The Acts of the Apostles* (London: Methuen & Co. Ltd., 1901), xcivf.
10. Ibid., xcv.
11. Ibid.
12. Ibid.
13. William Barclay, *The Letters to the Galatians and Ephesians*, rev. ed. (Philadelphia: The Westminster Press, 1976), 146.
14. *The Interpreter's Bible*, Vol. 10 (Nashville: Abingdon Press, 1953), 661.
15. Ibid.
16. Barclay, *The Letters to the Galatians and Ephesians*, rev. ed., 146f.
17. Eusebius, *The History of the Church from Christ to Constantine* (Harmondsworth: Dorset Press, 1983), 11.
18. Ibid., 213.

19. Hans Lietzmann, A *History of the Early Church*, Vol. 2 (Cleveland: The World Publishing Company, 1963), 300.
20. Kenneth Scott Latourette, A *History of the Expansion of Christianity*, Vol. 1 (New York: Harper & Brothers Publishers, 1937), 116.
21. G. S. P. Freeman-Grenville, *The New Atlas of African History* (New York: Simon & Schuster, 1991), 26.
22. Latourette, A *History of the Expansion of Christianity*, Vol. 1, 116.
23. *Interpreter's Dictionary of the Bible* E–J (Nashville: Abingdon Press, 1962), 181.
24. Eusebius, *The History of the Church from Christ to Constantine*, II.3.1, 76.
25. *The Interpreter's Dictionary of the Bible*, 181.
26. Rackham, *The Acts of the Apostles*, xcix.
27. Bultmann, *Theology of the New Testament*, Vol. II, 101.
28. Bruce, *Commentary on the Book of the Acts*, 244.
29. Ibid.
30. *Collins Concise Dictionary of the English Language*, 528.
31. Browning, A *Dictionary of the Bible*, 275.
32. Rudolf Bultmann, *Theology of the New Testament*, Vol. III (New York: Charles Scribner's Sons, 1955), 104.
33. Ibid., 101.
34. Ibid., 102.
35. Ibid.
36. Ibid.
37. Ibid.
38. Eusebius, *The History of the Church*, Book 3, 128.
39. Bultmann, *Theology of the New Testament*, Vol. III, 108. See also Did. 11, Herm. Mand. XI.
40. Ibid.
41. Cyril C. Richardson, ed., *Early Christian Fathers*, Vol. I (Philadelphia: The Westminster Press, MCMLIII), 95.
42. C. K. Barrett, *The Pastoral Epistles* (Oxford: The Clarendon Press, 1963), 71.
43. Ibid., 16.
44. Bultmann, *Theology of the New Testament*, Vol. III, 104f. See also Pastoral Letters, Did., Herm.
45. Ibid., 108.
46. Eusebius, *The History of the Church from Christ to Constantine*, Book 3, 118.
47. Alan Richardson, ed., *The Early Christian Fathers* (Oxford: Oxford University Press, 1969), 90.
48. Richardson, ed., *Early Christian Fathers*, Vol. I, 76.
49. Richardson, ed., *Early Christian Fathers*, Vol. I, 20.
50. Ibid., 20.
51. Ibid.
52. Ibid., 75.
53. Ibid., 88.

54. Bultmann, *Theology of the New Testament*, Vol. III, 110.
55. Ibid.
56. Richardson, *Early Christian Fathers*, Vol. I, 20.
57. Latourette, *A History of the Expansion of Christianity*, Vol. I, 116.
58. Ibid.
59. Edwin Charles Dargan, *A History of Preaching*, Vol. 1 (New York: Hodder & Stoughton, George H. Duran, Co., 1905), 106.

Chapter 13: The Sacraments

1. Browning, *A Dictionary of the Bible*, 329.
2. J. Stevenson, ed., *A New Eusebius* (London: S.P.C.K, 1970), 14.
3. Browning, *A Dictionary of the Bible*, 329.
4. Harvey, *A Handbook of Theological Terms*, 211.
5. Browning, *A Dictionary of the Bible*, 329.
6. Ibid., 329f.
7. Harvey, *A Handbook of Theological Terms*, 212.
8. Donald M. Baillie, *The Theology of The Sacraments* (New York: Charles Scribner's Sons, 1957), 80.
9. H. Grady Hardin, Joseph D. Quillian Jr., and James F. White, *The Celebration of the Gospel* (Nashville: Abingdon Press, 1964), 110.
10. Ibid., 111.
11. Baillie, *The Theology of the Sacraments*, 88.
12. Hardin, Quillian, White, *The Celebration of the Gospel*, 111.
13. Joachim Jeremias, *The Origins of Infant Baptism* (London: SCM Press LTD, 1963), 29.
14. Oscar Cullmann, *Baptism in the New Testament* (London: SCM Press LTD, 1964), 25.
15. Ibid., 46.
16. *The Journal of John Wesley* (Christian Classics Ethereal Library, https://www.ccel.org/ccel/wesley/journal.vi.ii.xvi.html).
17. Hardin, Quillian, White, *The Celebration of the Gospel*, 111.
18. Ibid., 120.
19. Ibid., 121.
20. Ibid., 121f.
21. Ibid., 121.
22. Ibid., 127.
23. *Collins Concise Dictionary of the English Language*, 521.
24. Hardin, Quillian, White, *The Celebration of the Gospel*, 127.
25. Ibid., 129.

Chapter 14: Eschatology

1. Browning, *A Dictionary of the Bible*, 120.
2. Hendricks et al., *Christian Word Book*, 98.
3. Kwesi A. Dickson and Paul Ellingworth, eds., *Biblical Revelation and African Beliefs* (London: Letterworth Press, 1970), 159ff.

4. Ibid., 168.
5. Michael Gelfand, *African Crucible: An ethico-religious study with special reference to the Shona-speaking people* (Cape: The Rustica Press, 1961), 54.
6. Ibid., 7.
7. Mbiti, *African Religions and Philosophy*, 2nd ed., 155.
8. Parratt, *Reinventing Christianity*, 97.
9. Ibid., 98, Footnote 83.
10. Ibid.
11. William Barclay, *The Letters of the Philippians, Colossians, and Thessalonians*, rev. ed. (Louisville: Westminster Press, 1975), 204.
12. Hendricks et al., *Christian Word Book*, 98.
13. Ibid., 99.
14. Ehrman, *The New Testament*, 61.
15. Hendricks et al., *Christian Word Book*, 99.
16. Abbott-Smith, *A Manual Greek Lexicon of the New Testament*, 347.
17. Vine, *An Expository Dictionary of New Testament Words*, 208.
18. Abbott-Smith, *A Manual Greek Lexicon of the New Testament*, 347.
19. Barclay, *The Letters to the Philippians, Colossians, and Thessalonians*, 203.
20. William J. Abraham, *The Logic Evangelism* (Grand Rapids: William B. Eerdmans Publishing Company, 1989), 92.

CPSIA information can be obtained
at www.ICGtesting.com
Printed in the USA
FSOW04n0215151217
41914FS